NEIL: A LONG JOURNEY HOME

A Memoir
by Judy Cowart

Autumn, 1983
Portland, Oregon

NEIL: A LONG JOURNEY HOME

The characters and events in this book are true.

Summary: Suffering from PMS and Panic Attacks, Judy is forced to seek medical help and ends up in a mental hospital where she meets Neil — the man of her childhood dreams — fifteen years too late. But he dies, and the pain is excruciating, until God intervenes with a few well-chosen words.

[1. Christianity, visions. 2. Psychiatry, Mental Hospitals. 3. Love, Friendship — Nonfiction]

Fonts — Text: Bookman Old Style. [160 pages]

INTRODUCTION

The house was new when I moved in. The walls were clean, bright, and cheery. I know they must have been. It's almost impossible to believe that now.

"Why do you keep painting the walls black?"

At some point the fires started. In the walls, in the foundation, in the attic. Nowhere you could really see. You just wake up one morning and find a patch of black soot staining the wallpaper. You spend all morning patching it.

"Why do you keep painting the walls black?"

After a while the wallpaper becomes too much effort. Then you keep a can of white paint handy to touch things up. Especially before company comes. But you can't hide it, the graying ashes, the blackening soot. People start talking. Just to each other, though, and they look at you sideways.

"Why do you keep painting the walls black?"

It comes to the place where you spend nearly every waking hour, nearly all your energy fighting it. Painting, whitewashing, trying to make it a decent place to live. But it's a losing battle. Desperation forces you to abandon certain rooms. Exhaustion causes you to cancel appointments. You cry out for help.

"Why do you keep painting the walls black?"

It's terrifying. The soot, the smell of ashes. You try to explain to people about the fires, but they don't listen. They can't see them and refuse to believe. Your best friends don't know what to believe. Most others act as if you were deliberately setting them. And the soot slowly begins to cover everything. The walls — you haven't the energy to paint anymore. The furnishings, the floor, until you are sitting and lying in the smutty stuff. And the windows — shutting out the light, leaving no hope, only darkness.

"Why do you keep painting the walls black?"

And they keep asking, asking, asking...

Logan Cowart[1]

---

[1] I wrote this about 1982 to express my idea of what Judy might be feeling. She said that I "got it", and used it as an introduction in her typed draft.   Logan.

PROLOGUE

REFLECTIONS FROM A HOSPITAL BED
IN A PSYCHIATRIC HOSPITAL

As I want for sleep to come,
Elusive feeling of calm,
I reflect ... what brought me here
To this place in time?

Are my feelings, my deep dark feelings,
Depression, blackness, pain, futility,
Are these hormonal? Medicine induced?
Or is there something buried, clawing its way out?

And God, where is He in all of this?
"Why standest Thou afar off, Lord?"
Ah, sweet child, I'm not afar off, but near.
I am what brought you to this place in time.

Why, why, why all this pain?
Not only to me, but to my loved ones?
I feel so useless, foolish, and weak.
"Yes, but in your weakness, I am made strong.
              You'll see ... have hope."

"... but those who hope in the Lord will renew their strength. They will soar on wings like eagles; they will run and not grow weary, they will walk and not be faint." (Is. 40:31)

I wrote the above my first night at Riverside Psychiatric Hospital while I waited for the sleeping pill to take effect. They had put me in a room where I could be alone the first night, and the best term I can use to describe my feelings at that time is shell-shocked. I couldn't believe I was in a psychiatric hospital — me — with all these "crazy people." Eventually, I was to find that these people weren't "crazy" — just people fighting battles much the same as mine, though theirs were more severe.

My problem began three years before with the birth of my son. Apparently, my hormones never righted themselves, which resulted in a condition only recently identified as "pre-menstrual syndrome." The first year, I kept thinking I'd soon overcome these "baby blues" if only I could get enough rest. After that, since my symptoms (depression, anxiety, irritability, fatigue) were cyclical and I had two or more good weeks between a week or so of "Mr. Hyde" behavior, I wasn't very motivated to seek help.

Eventually, however, the condition got progressively worse and was impossible to control, particularly since I had no idea what it was. The tension of not knowing what was going on in my body fed the tension already there. When I started having panic attacks, I was forced to seek help.

As I look back, I can see that God was leading me, though to me, at the time, it was all a black whirlpool that I couldn't escape. Just in time, I was led to a doctor who knew exactly what was wrong and what to do for me. I was hospitalized at Woodland Park Hospital for five days while tests were run and a psychiatric evaluation performed. I was pronounced sound in the mind and in touch with reality; put on a high protein, low sodium diet (the procedure for those who have premenstrual syndrome); and given tranquilizers to help cope with the symptoms, since I was told I would feel not much better for 2-4 months.

So, I was sent home, everyone happy that the mystery of my strange behavior was solved. But, alas, I could not cope. Two-to-four months seemed an eternity to me. I was high-strung, wondering when my next anxiety attack would hit. I didn't have the freedom to eat what I wanted anymore, and it seemed that everything had sodium in it. I couldn't take care of my son or do laundry, or simple household tasks. I spent hours crying. I had developed a reactive depression.

By the time the psychiatrist, Dr. Larsen, (a blonde Rosey Grier) saw me again, I was frightened, confused, and dull from too many tranquilizers. When I told him I just wanted to die, the decision was made that I should be checked into Riverside. He wanted to give me an anti-depressant in a large dosage right away, and he wanted my blood pressure continually monitored by people who are familiar with that type of medication.

And so it was that I met Neil.

1

I met Neil my first evening at Riverside. I had been admitted in the morning but had stayed in my room the whole day, afraid and depressed. Only the need for a tranquilizer about 5:00 in the evening forced me down to the nurse's station.

I was introduced to Shelli, the "med nurse," who gave me my tranquilizer (Xanax); and Barbara, one of the therapists gently led me to the dayroom (rather against my will) where a community meeting was just beginning. (I was to find that there were two community meetings a day — one in the morning and one in the evening — for the purpose of letting the patients know what activities to expect and what was new in policies, etc. It also gave the patients an opportunity to complain about a leaky faucet in their rooms or offer suggestions for improvements in living conditions.)

I was the last to arrive, and as I sat in a chair near the door, Neil was the first person I saw. There were perhaps a dozen people sitting in a circle of chairs and couches, and Neil was sitting on a couch directly across the room from me. He had been sitting back with his arms folded against his chest and his feet stretched out in front of him, ankles crossed.

At my entrance, however, he startled, putting his hands on the couch on either side of his hips, mouth open, almost gaping. As I sat down, I looked down at myself, making sure I was properly dressed. And I marveled that my body looked the same as it always had. My body that had betrayed me internally looked, on the outside, just like it did before this madness had come over me.

When I looked back up at Neil, he was still staring. I thought to myself: He looks so normal; I wonder why he's here. He had dark, curly, rather unruly hair, and haunted hazel eyes. He reminded me somewhat of Neil Diamond, except that he had shorter hair and his nose was a bit larger. He also had a straight, thick, black Italian-type moustache. I remember thinking that any girl would consider him a real "hunk." He had very broad shoulders and was perhaps 5'10" to 6' tall. He told me later that he weighed 199 lbs., and that he played football in high school. He was dressed in jeans, a navy blue t-shirt, and blue and white tennis shoes — his regular wardrobe — indeed, most everyone's regular wardrobe in the hospital.

Barbara introduced me as the new patient, and everyone then took turns introducing themselves. When it was Neil's turn, he was still studying me and said his name almost as an afterthought. The rest of the people were of all ages and sizes and shapes — all looking pretty non-threatening, so I began to relax.

I don't remember much about that first evening, except that Logan and Leighton, my husband and son, came to visit. A resident doctor came and took my health history and gave me a physical exam. And Barbara showed the movie, "9 to 5," in the dayroom. But I just took a sleeping pill early, went to bed and hoped I'd sleep forever.

2

How is it that when you first see someone, their spirit soars out to you, and you take them to your heart? That's how it was with Neil. Though we didn't have our first conversation for several days, I could tell he was someone desperately seeking answers. He was always busy, busy, busy. He reminded me of the Mad Hatter[2], always late for a very important date. He attacked all his tasks with a vengeance. He seemed driven and very intense about everything. Yet, I could also tell he was a kind, gentle, genuinely good person. So many times he showed these qualities, and they seemed to come so naturally, so second-nature. I remember thinking (I suppose because I'm a mother): You can tell he's been raised right.

I think it was the second morning I was in the hospital that he led Letha back to her room from the cafeteria. I was sitting across the table from them when Letha, an elderly woman — perhaps 75 years old — put her hand on Neil's arm and said, "I wonder if you'd ask that therapist to help me back to my room? I'm feeling a little dizzy."

---

[2] Yes, she should have said "the White Rabbit." But in this context, a reference to "the Mad Hatter" is more reasonable.   Logan.

She was referring to the therapist who was with the patients from the West Unit. (They were the ones who were severely disturbed. I lived on the East Unit.)

Neil immediately offered to help her himself, put his arm around her, and led her back. When he came back to the cafeteria, he calmly disposed of her tray and finished his own meal.

Pattie was a 26-year-old woman with a 3-year-old mind. I found myself responding to her much as I did to my son. She was in the hospital for management of her anger. I learned early on that she needed her space; she didn't want anyone to get physically close to her — except Neil. It was obvious to all that she had a real crush on Neil. He could very easily have ignored her or been impatient with her and we would all have understood. But, he never acted embarrassed about her attentions, and in a kind and older brotherly sort of way was very courteous with her. I remember he tried to show her how to play pool during a pool tournament, a patient activity we were having one evening. She still didn't do very well, but I admired Neil's thoughtfulness and patience.

On the Saturday morning after I was admitted, Neil sat across from me at breakfast. After the perfunctory good mornings, we ate silently for several minutes. When he started studying me, as he had that first time in the community meeting, I got uncomfortable. It was as if he were silently asking, "Who _are_ you, anyway?" Throughout my month-long stay in the hospital, Neil eyed me that way often, and it wasn't long before I simply accepted that behavior as a part of Neil and forgot about it.

But that morning, I felt compelled to start a conversation to put a halt to his study of me. I felt like a bug under a microscope.

I commented that it was a nice morning, and he agreed. Silence. More staring. I asked him if he were going to the Yamhill Market — the patient outing for the day.

"Yeah," he nodded. "Are you?"

"No, I'm going home for a couple of hours — to see how I feel about being there."

Neil nodded again slowly and said softly, "Ah," rather like a professor comprehending a difficult concept. "Do you live alone?"

"Oh no," I said in surprise. "I live with my husband and three-year-old son."

Neil's eyebrows went up. "Ah," he said again. He took a bite of egg. "I thought you lived alone."

We each pondered silently how he could have come to that conclusion. I wondered especially, since we hadn't talked before. I finally asked, "Why did you think I lived alone?"

Neil really enjoyed eating, and this particular meal he was eating with gusto. "Mmmm..." He said, chewing on a big bite of toast, "I guess it was something you said in group about being alone all the time."

It was then that I remembered describing my depression at a group therapy session. I said I had just stayed at home all the time and wanted to be alone. I didn't want to reach out to anyone for help.

"Ah," Neil said again. "That's a classic symptom of depression. It was very natural for you to feel that way."

"Really?" I said, suddenly feeling a little more normal.

"Yeah," Neil chewed his bacon and took a drink of milk.

It was soon time for Logan to pick me up, so I excused myself. Neil stood up as I left, a courtesy I hadn't seen in years.

"Have a good morning," I said, smiling.

"Uh, thanks...uh...You have a good morning, too," he responded, getting back to his meal right away.

So, what, I wondered, in the rare moments when my whole existence wasn't concentrated on holding mind and body together, was Neil doing here?

I found out the next evening.

3

The next evening was a Sunday evening, and I was practically the only patient on the East Unit. Most of the others had passes to see their families or just to take a break away from the hospital. I had spent that afternoon at home, and though I enjoyed the familiar surroundings, it had taken all my energy just to cope. I was glad to be back at the hospital.

My anti-depressant was working well. Although thinking about food made me nauseous, and anxiety was my constant companion, and I felt dizzy much of the time, I had managed to string together a couple of good days, mood-wise. I was bored, so I went down to the dayroom to see what was on television.

Sixty Minutes was on, and I got absorbed in a story about an Oregon man who, years after coming back from Vietnam, had brutally butchered his girl-friend and nearly murdered her roommate. His defense was that he had gone into a spell, because of Vietnam, where he didn't know what he was doing — something called "delayed stress syndrome."

I was all alone until halfway into the segment, Neil came in. He paced around, smoking a cigarette, going in and out of the room. I didn't pay much attention to him; my impression was that he had his mind on something else.

When there was mentioned a possible mistake in military records, Neil exploded.

"Military records?! Military records!" His voice got shrill. "I can't believe they're hanging this guy on the reliability of military records! What a lot of sh--!"

I must have looked shocked, because he immediately apologized for his language. It wasn't his profanity that had shocked me; it was the suddenness of his emotional outburst.

"I'm gonna sue this government, you know it? It's corrupt. It caused my nervous breakdown, it's caused my depression; and I'm gonna bring the Portland police down with it, too! They're all gonna wish they'd never heard of Neil McCarthy!"

He ranted a little more about injustice and big government and the little guy, and I began to realize that now my curiosity about why Neil was in the hospital was going to be satisfied.

When he paused to put out his cigarette in the ash tray that was on the end table next to me, I ventured, "You had a nervous breakdown, Neil?"

He must have sensed my interest and willingness to listen, because he sat down, lit another cigarette, and started in on his story with an air of having told it many times before.

I'm not sure of the time frame of his story; and much of the order is confused, because after that night he didn't want to talk about it much. And while he was telling it, I didn't want to interrupt with questions, mostly because it became obvious he needed to talk about it, and also I didn't want to appear nosey.

It seems that in the latter part of 1968, Neil was drafted against his will. He told me later that he signed up to go to Vietnam only because it would get him out of the military sooner.

While in Vietnam he became severely depressed. He told his commanding officer he needed some rest and recreation or to see a chaplain, but his commanding officer told him he was there to do a job and he'd better do it. One day, he said, he thought his mind would snap, and he told his commanding officer that he couldn't do "it" anymore. (He never told me what "it" was, or any of his activities in Vietnam.) His commanding officer told him all he had was two months left, and he'd better hold out until then.

The next day, though, his whole company was on an Army jet to Oakland. President Nixon was starting to pull the troops out, decreasing the U.S. involvement in the war. Three days later, Neil was discharged from the Army. That was June 9, 1970. Neil could tell me how long he was in the Army, down to the minute.

The shock was tremendous. He said he wandered around Oakland several days. A couple of the guys in his company told him he'd better get some help, but he didn't know where to turn.

Finally, he decided to go up to Tacoma where his brother was stationed in the Air Force. Here is where the story got fuzzy. Somehow or another he ended up at Ft. Steilacoom, where he had his nervous breakdown. They patched him up, he said, and got him out as soon as they could. For 13 years he was in and out of 22 hospitals and/or mental institutions.

By this time he was talking calmly and conversationally, as if he were talking about his last summer's vacation. I was the one in shock.

"So how did you end up here?" I asked, trying not to let my feelings show and make him uncomfortable.

Again, the details are fuzzy, but he had heard that the V.A. Hospital in Portland might be able to help him. Instead, he got the "royal run-around," as he put it, and wasn't even able to see a psychiatrist. He was put on an anti-depressant, however, but they didn't work. He said he wasn't any happier, and he couldn't think straight.

He had been on Social Security disability all this time and was having some problem with the Portland office. It gets unclear again, but my understanding of the story is that he felt they were giving him the "royal run-around," too. After several trips to the office, he lost control. He said the milling crowd in the room made him nervous, and the depression and frustration got the better of him. He pushed two employees out of their chairs, and when their supervisor, "A wimpy man with a bad back" put his arms around Neil's arms and chest from behind and yelled, "Neil, get a hold of yourself," Neil said he just lost it. He sprung the guy off him like he was the Incredible Hulk, knocking the supervisor against a file cabinet. Neil then proceeded to push himself roughly through the crowd and out the door.

"I felt like I was going to suffocate; I was desperate and didn't know what to do. So, I went next door to this bar and got drunk. Only, I was on those anti-depressants and I passed out. When I woke up, I was in the back seat of a police car."

Neil was charged with assault and resisting arrest. This was when he started ranting again, and the worry lines, which I was going to see regularly, appeared on his forehead.

"They said it took four policemen to subdue me! How could it? I was passed out! Four policemen perjured themselves and said I was sober and resisted arrest!"

Neil had a public defender since he couldn't afford a lawyer, and she advised him to enter a no-contest plea as a plea bargaining effort. She told him that since it was his first offense, he'd probably just be fined or put on probation.

"I had to decide in two hours. God, I was depressed, and I couldn't think. It really went against my grain to plead no-contest to the resisting arrest charge, but my lawyer said I probably wouldn't win it and she applied a lot of pressure, so I said okay."

The judge sentenced Neil to a year in jail.

"Man, I was bombed out. I couldn't believe it. I told him I wanted a new lawyer. My friend, Vaughn, posted bail, and I went to live with him."

That was when he started thinking about suicide. "I was cornering in on suicide, lying on the couch, thinking how I was gonna do it when this commercial for Care Unit came on."

(I laughed inside myself at this point, because when I was home and depressed, I had seen the same commercial on television and wished it was advertising a hospital for PMS patients.)

Neil called Care Unit, asking if they had facilities for depressed people. They suggested Riverside. When he called Riverside, the girl told him they didn't accept Medicare insurance and to try Providence Hospital's psychiatric unit.

"But she took my name and number and told me they'd work something out if Providence didn't work out. I called Providence, and they said I couldn't just check myself in; I'd have to be admitted by one of their psychiatrists. By that time, I felt like I was just getting another royal run-around, so I went to sleep. That night, Shelli (the med nurse) called and asked how I was doing. When I told her about Providence, she said Riverside <u>does</u> accept Medicare and if I wanted to, I could come right then and they'd admit me and assign me to a psychiatrist. So I came — it was about 10:00 at night."

An hour or more had gone by, Sixty Minutes long forgotten. I felt wrung out. How could someone feel so badly for so long and still cope? I'd been depressed on and off for three years and was ready to throw in the towel. He must have been here awhile and been getting excellent care.

"Who's your doctor?" I asked him.

"Dr. Larsen."

"Mine, too!"

"Yeah, he's the best," Neil said, stretching his arms above his head. "He's given me some meds that have really helped. And he's straight with you — no bull."

"How long have you been here?" I asked.

"I came in last Saturday night."

Eight days ago! I was admitted on the Wednesday following his Saturday admission. Only four days later! And he seemed so normal! Truly I was in the presence of a master survivor.

4

After that Sunday evening, Neil and I developed an interesting relationship. It was obvious to me from the beginning that socially, he was stuck back at twenty years old. His overtures of friendship took on an approach-avoidance situation.

If he wanted me to go for a walk, the scenario usually went like this:

Neil: "I think I'll go for a walk today about 2:30."

Me: "That sounds like a good idea."

Neil: "Are you going to be doing anything then?"

Me: "No, probably not."

Neil: "Oh."

Pause.

Depending on who couldn't stand the silence anymore (usually me), one of us would suggest a walk together, then we'd agree to meet in the lobby for a walk.

Or, if he did take the initiative to ask if I wanted him to get me something at the store or watch a football game with him, he usually stammered it out in such a way that I'd agree to what he wanted, whether I originally wanted to or not. And on the occasions when I had to refuse, though I went out of my way to spare his feelings, he'd usually look at me for a minute, slowly say "Ah ... Okay," and walk away, looking (to me) dejected. Then he'd ignore me for a day or so. I'd feel like a real jerk.

I remember one evening we were watching a movie in the dayroom. Neil was sitting on one end of the couch; I was on the other end, closest to the television. He left and came back a few minutes later with two cartons of milk. After several minutes of holding them, he finally thrust one at me saying, "Does anybody want some milk?"

I felt like looking all around me for the non-existent people he could be offering it to, but I didn't. I didn't want that milk, but I took it, thanked him profusely, and choked it down.

Our walks usually took on a pattern of Neil outlining his plans to get back at the government or the justice system. They varied day to day from forming a group of disgruntled veterans to overthrow the military system, to putting ads in newspapers all over the country to find his old company from Vietnam to testify when he sued the government. He ranted on and on about how the Portland police were just waiting for him to get out of the hospital so they could move him through a kangaroo court.

He'd enumerate over and over how much money the government had had to spend on him through welfare, social security, and Medicare, because they "f---ed up" and then bring up how a single mother had to beg for food stamps. The injustice of it all infuriated him.

I usually just listened, taking what he said with a grain of salt, knowing he needed to talk. To me, he was Don Quixote, fighting windmills. I didn't know how much was true and how much was just a distortion of reality as he saw it. I knew depression sometimes played tricks with how a person perceives the world, so I usually didn't say much, because I had seen him react with anger when anyone else tried to dissuade him. Though I knew he wouldn't hurt me physically, my nature is usually to avoid any angry confrontation at all costs, so I kept silent. I just hoped that by talking about it, he'd get all the hate and revenge out of his system.

I was taking this interest in Neil, I decided, because I wanted him to trust me. I could tell he hadn't trusted anybody as a friend for a long time. Out of the hospital, we wouldn't have had enough in common to hold a strong friendship together. Our lifestyles were completely different, our backgrounds very divergent. We moved in such completely different circles, we wouldn't have even met outside the hospital. But, in the hospital, we were the only two the same age (33), we enjoyed the same kind of movies, we liked watching football on television, we had the same doctor, we swapped similar depression stories, and we liked to walk. We also had a lot to learn from each other, and I think we both sensed it. If I could only get him to trust me more...

5

On my second week in the hospital, Dr. Larsen was so pleased with the progress I was making on the anti-depressant that he decided to increase it. This proved to be both a mistake and bad timing.

On the second evening on my new dosage, I barely got back from the cafeteria. The walls and floor seemed to shift from side to side and I felt faint and nauseous. Shelli took one look at me and called the resident doctor. He gave me a general exam, took my blood pressure, and called Dr. Larsen. It was decided that my anti-depressant be stopped, and I was given Anti-Vert, a drug to decrease the extreme vertigo from which I was suffering.

For three days I laid on my bed, feeling like I was on a boat in a very bad storm. If I turned my head, my stomach would lurch. Dr. Larsen came and went, assuring me I'd feel better soon, but I told him I just wanted to die. He also told me a virus was going around the hospital with the same symptoms (how could I be so lucky?), but he was 90% sure this was as a result of my increased medication, because my blood pressure was 80/50. When a blood test showed that my white blood cell count was up, he attributed my symptoms to both the medication and the virus.

On the fourth morning after my illness had first begun, I found I could sit, stand, and walk around my room, all without stumbling too much. Seeking some human companionship that wasn't going to poke needles in me or take my vital signs, I staggered into the dayroom where a community meeting was just getting started, dragging a chair behind me.

Neil was nearest the doorway, and when he caught sight of me, he jumped up, moved his chair to make room for my chair, and then he positioned it in the circle for me. All the while we held a whispered conversation.

"Where have you been?" he asked, grabbing my chair.

"I've been sick," I whispered back.

"Because of your meds?"

"Yeah, and some kind of flu, too."

"Ah," he said as I was seating myself. "I was wondering why you were hiding out in your room. I was afraid it was something I said."

A surprised shake of my head was the only response I could make, because the meeting had already begun.

Oh, Neil, I thought to myself. How could you think that? Do you still trust me so little? Has that happened to you before?

6

Later that morning there was a group therapy session that was to change the entire climate of our friendship.

I was late for that session because I was the last to see Dr. Larsen that day, and he was running late. He wanted to start me on a reduced dosage of the anti-depressant again, the whole dosage to be taken at bed-time; so that if it made me dizzy, I'd be dizzy when I was asleep. We also dickered about how much Xanax (tranquilizer) I should be taking and how often. We discussed my blood pressure and lack of appetite. All in all, it was a session that gave me a lot to think about, so when I went into the dayroom, my mind was still on Dr. Larsen.

There were perhaps six patients there, and Roger, the therapist, was talking to Neil about making friends. I went on wondering if taking my medication would make me sick again until Roger said, "What about the people here, Neil? Is there anybody in this group you'd like to know better?"

I started rubbing my eyes, wondering if there would be time to take a nap after group therapy before I had to have lunch.

Neil looked around, hesitated, and then said, "I guess I'd like to know Judy better, because she's always in bed."

There was a stunned silence. The hand that was rubbing my eyes stopped in mid-rub. Even Roger, who I'm sure thought he'd heard everything, was speechless. Finally, there was some nervous laughter, and I said, in surprise, "Thanks a lot, Neil! That's a real ego boost!"

Neil smiled a little, stretched his hands out and said, "I wasn't thinking about sex ... it's just that ... well ... you've been sick, and I haven't seen you ... I didn't mean ... oh, sh--!"

It was all downhill after that. Roger was trying to pin Neil down to something specific he could do to get to know me better. It went on and on, and I felt more and more uncomfortable. I felt like I was in junior high, and some boy was being forced to dance with me.

Finally, Neil burst out, "I don't know! All the girls I've ever met were in bars! I feel really awkward about this."

He pointed at me. "She's a married woman. I just feel like her husband would tell me to stay away from his wife." He started rubbing his forehead. "I don't want to talk about this anymore!"

Roger went on relentlessly, and I wanted to leave. It was obvious Neil was feeling cornered. Tension was running high. After a while, Neil wasn't talking at all. He was just immobile, slouched in his chair, one hand on his eyebrows, eyes down, his face a mask of pain. I thought it was going to go on forever. I found myself wondering if I would be able to talk the med nurse into an early Xanax dose.

Finally, Roger asked me for a response. I shrugged my shoulders. After a moment of thought, I began in a strained, nervous voice, "It makes me feel good that Neil wants to know me better ..."

"Tell Neil," Roger interrupted.

I took a deep breath. "Neil," I repeated, "It makes me feel good that you want to get to know me better. I have friends who are men that aren't a threat to my marriage. Honestly, anybody who knows my husband at all knows he's not the jealous type. Our friendship wouldn't bother him at all."

I stopped to gather my thoughts. "I'd like to get to know you better, too. I want you to know that you face absolutely no risk with me. I like you." By then I was feeling shaky and so sorry for Neil.

"Neil?" Roger said. "Any response?"

Neil just sat huddled in his chair as before. A tear ran unchecked down his cheek.

When the session ended at last, I was a ball of indecision. If I hadn't been the object of this painful situation, wild horses couldn't have kept me from staying behind and offering Neil my support. I would have done that for anyone who had just gone through what Neil had; I was furious with Roger for having leaned so hard. Yet, I knew if I stayed behind, I'd just make the whole situation worse.

"I feel so bad!" I wailed to Mary, my roommate, that afternoon. She was a 53-year-old school teacher, who had also been at group. Mary had been at River-side on and off for several years. I never did know what her problem was, and I don't think she knew either.

Nevertheless, she had a marvelous sense of humor; she was extremely perceptive; and to say she was intelligent is an understatement. She reminded me in both looks and actions of the television character, Maude; though Mary looked older and more emotion-torn.

She had just filled me in on the beginning of the group therapy that I had missed that morning. Roger had asked if anyone wanted to bring up any problems, and after "an eternity" Bob, another patient, mentioned the subject of friendships and making friends, and they had talked about that briefly. Neil contributed the comment that he felt like he didn't belong in society anywhere because he had lost the ability to make friends. So, it appears, Roger zeroed in on Neil.

Mary had stayed behind to talk to Neil, "but he didn't say much," she said. "He just said he felt like he'd made a fool of himself and he couldn't face anybody and got up and left." That's when I wailed my frustration to her.

"Oh, I wouldn't worry about it too much," she said, rifling through her purse for her car keys. "We all have our painful moments here. Neil will get over it. But, I am mad at Roger — he's always going for blood."

I was a bundle of nerves that whole day. I was afraid if I ran into Neil, he'd think I was waiting around for an overture of friendship. And I was afraid if I stayed away from him, he'd think I was avoiding him.

I needn't have worried that day. Neil disappeared until late that night. One of the three showers on the East Unit opened directly across from the nurses' station, and when I came out of it about 10:30,

Shelli was scolding Neil for staying out so late and long without signing out.

"I know you're not the kind to just go running off, so I didn't call the police. But, we're responsible for you here, Neil, and it was making all of us real nervous. A lot of other people would have been confined to their rooms for something like that."

I didn't wait around to hear his response; I ducked into my room before he could turn around and see me.

The next day was Saturday, and I went home for several hours. I poured the story out to Logan. We laughed briefly over the mental image of my sweet-natured, slow-to-anger, 5'8" husband punching out the hulk that was Neil.

"Just treat him naturally, Jude," Logan advised me. "Just act like it didn't happen, and he'll probably come to feel more comfortable with you." It turned out to be excellent advice.

I saw Neil just once that evening. He was sitting in a chair at the nurses' station, having his vital signs taken. We saw each other at the same time. I was on my way to the dayroom to make a phone call. He looked down quickly at his lap.

I hesitated, then called up what little courage I had at the moment and marched past him, squeezing his shoulder gently as I went by.

"Hi, Neil," I said in what I hoped was a bright, cheerful voice.

I had taken four or five steps before I heard his muffled "hi." That was all.

The next day was Sunday, and as was usual for a weekend morning community meeting, there were few of us there.

Besides Neil and myself, there were Roger ("the Hun" I was beginning to call him in my thoughts), Jo-Anne, a middle-aged new patient; Marvin, Neil's room-mate; and Kathy, who had been transferred from the West Unit during my illness in bed.

Marvin was 27 years old and had been in and out of the hospital for several months for severe de-pression. He was slightly built, about 5'10" with light brown hair and a scraggly beard that reached almost to his chest. He was a very quiet person, and this was the first time I had seen him alert in any kind of meet-ing, because he had been having shock therapy. Usu-ally, he'd just stare ahead or fall asleep. He was obvi-ously feeling a lot better.

The reason for Kathy's transfer from the West Unit is a mystery to me to this day. She was an attrac-tive 37-year-old who acted about 15. She had a very rapid way of talking that made you feel like you were being hit by machine-gun fire. When I listened to her, some of the words made their target inside my brain for interpretation, but she talked so fast that the rest of her words simply bounced off my head and fell by the wayside. It was also obvious she had little touch with reality. I learned later that she had a type of schizophrenia. She didn't have multiple personalities; but for some reason, she couldn't deal with her world the way it was. So, to cope, she just made up her own world and tried to make everyone else live in it. One by one, I had heard during my illness, she had made en-emies of most of the other patients on the East Unit by making insensitive remarks. I hadn't had any contact with her until that morning.

"So what do you want to do this morning?" Roger the Hun was asking.

"Oh, Marvin and I are going for a walk down to Sellwood Park," Kathy fired off quickly, hanging on Marvin's arm. "He needs to get out! I keep telling him he needs exercise. It'll make him feel so much better. Don't you think so, Roger?" She smiled brightly.

"Have you thought of asking any of the others here if they'd like to go, too?" Roger asked.

Kathy sat back, brow furrowed. Marvin leaned over Kathy, disentangling himself from her and said, "Neil, why don't you come, too?"

Neil looked up at me, and we locked gazes. Finally, I looked at Marvin and said, "I'd like to go with you and Kathy, Marvin."

Neil sighed. Then he looked back at Marvin. "Yeah, I'll go, too."

JoAnne had something else to do, so the four of us set out. First, Marvin and Neil walked side by side with Kathy in front of them, talking a mile a minute, and I walked behind. Then Kathy was walking with Marvin, and Neil was walking on the other side of Marvin, trampling somebody's bushes. After a while Marvin and Kathy were walking together and Neil walked ahead. I enjoyed bringing up the rear. While it was the most bizarre walk I had ever taken, I was somewhat insulated from Kathy's non-stop chatter, and I was noticing the pretty flowers and the warm sunshine — something that hadn't had my attention for a long time.

When we got to the park, Neil decided to walk some more around the park, and Kathy went with him. So Marvin and I sat down on a bench. I found out he was from Astoria, a coastal town on the northern-most tip of Oregon. He lived with his parents, and he had an older brother and sister. He also had a delightful dry sense of humor, and we had a nice chat. He had known Kathy when she had been at Riverside several months ago.

Soon Kathy was back. "Are you married?" she asked me.

"Yes," I nodded.

"So am I, but Gary and I are getting a divorce September 29, because he's in love with Carolyn, and I'm in love with Hank. But we're still all going to be good friends — all four of us — because of Mikey, our two-year-old son. We'll just all share him, because we're Christians. Gary and I have been married for 17 years, but he made me lose my confidence, because he was in the military, and we moved all over, so I had 12 break-downs. But, I'm getting better because the Lord gives me strength. Are you a religious person?"

"Uh, yes," was all I managed to say, stunned by the barrage of words.

"Isn't that wonderful? I had Mikey two years ago, but I had high blood pressure and got toxemia, so they took him by Cesarean section. I was so scared, because before Mikey, I had endometriosis, and I did-n't think I could have kids, but I had 11 operations, and now I have Mikey, my wonderful little son."

Marvin and I looked at each other. He was sup-pressing a smile behind his beard. Neil had returned, but he was pacing all around and back and forth, studying the ground and smoking a cigarette.

"Were you ever in the military, Neil?" Marvin asked in what looked to me an attempt to draw Neil into the conversation.

"Yeah, the Army," he spat out, vehemently.

"And proud of it!" I joked, hoping to lighten the tone of his answer.

It was a mistake.

"Proud? The Army can go to hell for all I care!" Neil slapped at a bug for emphasis. He went on ranting for a couple of sentences about what the Army could do with itself before I touched him on the arm.

"Neil," I said softly, hoping he wouldn't slap my hand off. "I was just joking."

He stopped with the suddenness of someone shutting off a faucet. He closed his eyes and took a deep breath.

"I'm sorry," I said, putting my hand back in my lap. Neil just nodded his head and started pacing again.

"Gary's a major." Kathy said, brightly. "I'm really proud of him. Could we go? I'm getting cold. Walking always warms me up. I know I should have worn a sweater, but when I wear a sweater when I walk, I always get too hot."

Like sheep, we followed her out of the park, while she rattled on about what made her too hot and what made her too cold.

Neil fell behind and started walking with me. We walked in silence for a while, and then I ventured another apology.

"Neil, I'm sorry I joked about your being proud to be in the Army. I know how strongly you feel about it, and that was really insensitive of me."

"Forget it," he said, grinding his cigarette butt into the sidewalk. "I ... uh ... don't like it when I get on my soap box like that. I hate myself when I bitch on it forever." He put his hands half-way into the front pockets of his jeans, and we walked in silence for another few minutes.

I told him that Logan had been drafted, too, but that he'd just missed having to go to Vietnam and spent most of the rest of his Army time in Colorado Springs.

"He didn't like the Army, either;" I told him. "He was supposed to be a medic, but he spent most of his time in the motor pool."

When I started talking about Logan, I noticed Neil stiffen. Sensing that was also a subject he was uncomfortable with, I dropped it.

Kathy and Marvin were ahead of us. Suddenly, Kathy turned.

"Neil?" she yelled. "What kind of flowers are those?" She was pointing to some gorgeous yellow and orange flowers in a yard we were passing.

"Uh ... I don't know," he answered, acting confused with the sudden change of subject. He looked over at me. "Do you know?"

"No, I'm not much good at identifying plants," I answered. "We should have Florence here. She could tell us."

Florence was about 70 years old. Her room was next-door to mine, and she and I took several walks together. Honestly, she could identify every flower we

passed. She was always after me to water the chrysan-
themums the church sent me.

"I remember when I was a little kid," Neil said,
looking up at the sky. "I saw these really deep purple
flowers. They were real little, and there was a bunch
of them all together. And I said to my mom, 'Look at
those pretty flowers!' And she said, 'Oh, Neil! Those are
weeds!'"

He smiled wryly. "At least I never had to weed
her garden; she never trusted me to know the difference between flowers and weeds."

I smiled at his story, and we walked along qui-
etly. Kathy and Marvin were way ahead of us, but we
could still hear Kathy dominating the conversation. I
was thinking how nice it felt to be outside and how
peaceful the neighborhood was that morning. I was
also starting to feel tired. It had been a 15-minute walk
to the park, and we weren't even half-way back yet.

"It's that way with people, isn't it?" Neil said,
strongly, his nostrils flaring.

I was startled both by what he said and that he
was speaking at all. I fumbled around for a meaning.
"Flowers and people?" I said at last.

"Yeah, some are flowers and some are weeds, ya
know? But who's to say who are flowers and who are
weeds? Some weeds are pretty, and they aren't hurting
anything by being there. Still, they're yanked out, even
when maybe they're prettier than the so-called flowers
around them."

Oh, Neil, I thought to myself, do you feel like a
weed? Do you feel yanked out?

We went on in silence for maybe ten steps and
then he asked me if I was getting tired. "We can sit

down, if you want." He looked at his watch. "There is nothing we have to get back for."

I told him I was doing okay and that I admired how busy he stayed at the hospital. I said that it probably did him a lot of good that he stayed so busy.

"Yeah, but I think maybe I stay too busy. I don't have enough time to think, you know? I'm gonna cut out some stuff that's not doing me any good. Like group ..." There was an awkward pause, then shaking his head he said, "I'm never going to group again."

Relieved that he'd brought it up, I told him how badly I had felt about Friday's group. I told him I hadn't known what to do about it and that I'd felt pushed on him.

"Maybe if you'd known Roger was going to make you think up specific ways to get to know me better, you'd have picked knowing Marvin better."

"Yeah, getting to know a married woman better is really limited, ya know? I didn't want your husband coming after me, and there's not a whole lot you can do in the hospital. I could say, 'Would you like to go to the cafeteria with me tonight — I'll pay — take care of the tip and everything,' but I'd feel silly. It's not me. I couldn't ask you to go to a show. We can't go to a bar. I mean ... God, I can't think of any ways to be friends with a married woman!"

"But, Neil," I broke in, "Aren't we already friends? Is the fact that I'm married that much of a barrier? We've taken walks together, eaten together; I enjoyed seeing Airplane with you in the dayroom the other night, and what about that Dallas football game we watched? Do you feel my husband breathing down your neck?"

He looked back suddenly, then at me and realized I was joking, and we both laughed.

I went on. "The rules have changed, I suppose, since we're both stuck at the hospital. If we were both just regular people on the street and you asked me to watch Airplane with you one evening, it would be totally inappropriate since I'm married ..."

"Yeah," he interrupted emphatically, gesturing with one hand. "You see?"

"<u>But</u>," I went on, pressing my point, "it would be inappropriate because you would be taking me away from my family. You would be excluding my husband and threatening, perhaps, the commitment I have to him. But here in the hospital, it's not <u>you</u> that is taking me away from my husband, it's the hospital taking me away from my husband. Both of us were here, and we both like movies, so you asked me to watch Airplane with you. I'm already away from my family, so it's just two friends watching a movie. That's all."

We were approaching the steps of the hospital. Neil stopped. "I've never had a friend that was a girl that I didn't ... you know ... want to date ... uh ... that was ... well, a sex object, you know?" He looked down, worry lines all over his forehead. "I'm having trouble with this."

I leaned on the handrail, sighed, and looked around. I suppose I was wishing an answer would just appear on the side of the building or up in the clouds. Finally I said, "I guess it all boils down to intention. You have no intention of breaking up my marriage. You have no intention of 'coming on' to me, right?"

He shook his head, quickly.

"Okay," I went on. "Why does my sex have to get in the way? Can't we just share the same things as two people while we're here?"

He didn't answer. Since it was time for lunch, we went on to the cafeteria. Marvin and Kathy were already there. She was telling him what foods gave her hives and what foods gave her rashes. Neil didn't say much, and Marvin and I managed some conversation around Kathy's chatter.

After they left, Neil asked, "Do you have friends that are men and your husband isn't jealous?"

"Oh, yes! Usually, we've shared those friends, but I have some friends that are men that I talk to more than Logan does, just because I have more in common with them."

I was puzzled. This seemed such an elementary concept to me. I was groping for words. Then Logan and Leighton came into the cafeteria. I was going home for a few hours that afternoon, and they had come looking for me.

When I introduced them to Neil and as they were shaking hands, Logan said, "I'm glad Judy has friends while she's here in the hospital."

I smiled in surprise and delight. What a wonderful and timely thing to say! I could have kissed him! Neil sat on my left, silent and brooding, looking defensive, as I finished up my meal and chatted with my family. After a couple of minutes, Leighton needed the services of a restroom, so Logan told me they'd meet me in the lobby.

"Now," I said after they were gone, "does he look like the kind of guy that would punch your lights out?"

Neil chuckled and relaxed. "No, I guess not."

"One time," I said with a smile of remembrance, "when I was at work, I ran into a guy I used to date. Since it was right around lunch time, he asked me to have lunch with him. And I did, without hesitation, because I was glad to see him and considered him my friend. That night, without hesitation, I told Logan about it, and he thought it was really nice that I had run into him again. Logan is just not the jealous type."

Neil looked up from his plate and fixed his gaze on a window directly across from us. "You must really have a lot of trust between you," he said wistfully, a catch in his voice.

"Yeah, we do," I answered slowly, and I thought to myself: Yeah, we really do. What a blessing I've taken for granted. Neil acts like this is so rare, and maybe it is.

Neil turned to me, pain written all over his face. "I've sat next to married women and had their husbands threaten me. I've sat next to unmarried women, and they've acted like I was trying to rape them."

"Oh, Neil!" I gasped, shocked. "That must have made you feel awfully inhibited!"

He just nodded and took another bite of his lunch. I wanted to cry. He looked confused and pitiful.

We sat in silence while he ate and I tried to think of something to comfort him. But I didn't know how to form the words. When I finished drinking my glass of milk, I turned to Neil and put my hand on his arm. "Look, Neil," I began, "I am very much in love with my husband and he is with me. My commitment is to him, and there is no one else for me in a romantic sense. There just isn't. But, as much as Logan and I mean to each other, he can't be all things to me, and I can't be all things to him. I <u>need</u> friends. We all need friends. I enjoy your company, and I'd like for you to be my friend." I stopped, thinking maybe I was getting a little preachy.

I got up. Neil followed me with his eyes. He had that look again, like I was the bug under the microscope. "I guess what I'm saying is that if you'd like me for a friend ... well ... you know where to find me." Neil wrinkled his brow. "Okay ... uh ... thanks."

I had to leave; I knew Logan was wondering what was taking me so long, particularly since I had no appetite and only ate two or three bites a meal.

I remember wondering as I walked down the hall on my way to the lobby if our talk had done any good. I hoped he understood, because I felt kind of silly about the whole thing. I also remember feeling really exhausted.

7

After that afternoon, Neil was different. He still had his cautious moments, but it was as if he'd learned the rules of friendship and now he could move freely within them. Gone was the hesitant, stammering Neil.

When I returned that evening, I was depressed and discouraged. Leighton had been cranky because we had had to wake him from his nap to get me back to the hospital on time. I rocked him, but not enough to suit either of us. I had felt claustrophobic in our truck. It was a long half-hour drive.

In the cafeteria, Mary was reading a newspaper across the table from Neil when I set my tray down next to Neil's. Before I had a chance to touch my chair, Neil jumped up, pulled my chair out, offered his arm, and said in mock soberness, looking down his nose at me, "would you care to join me for dinner?"

I stared at him in surprise for an instant; then suppressing a giggle, I answered, "But, of course!"

I took his arm and we sat down. Then we laughed, rolling in our seats. Mary looked over her glasses at us, then resumed reading. Clearly, she had seen weirder things in a psychiatric hospital.

A delightful sense of humor emerged in Neil. Most of it was about food and my lack of appetite.

"You know," he said once, pointing his fork in my direction, "A lot of people are Weight Watchers. But you're a food watcher." It was true. All I did was look at my food.

Another time, Janet, another patient of Dr. Larsen's, was also choking down food. We were swapping conversations we'd had with the doctor about our lack of appetite.

"He told me, 'You can have a Rolls Royce in mint condition, but if you don't put gas in it, it's not going to get out of the driveway. Eating properly is essential!'"

Janet finished the story with me word for word. She had gotten the same lecture.

"Yeah, well, tell him you're a compact model," Neil said, taking a bite of corn on the cob.

After a round of laughter, I told Neil I'd tell the doctor that Neil ate enough for all three of us.

"That's because Neil's a Mac Truck," said Marvin, unexpectedly. (Marvin always talked unexpectedly; you never knew when he was going to speak up.)

Neil laughed with the rest of us, stretched his arms above his head and offered, "Anytime you want a piggy-back ride, let me know. I'll get you out of the driveway."

Much of his humor had a you'd-have-to-be-there-to-understand-it quality. Once, in Arts and Crafts, we fantasized about having a five-year reunion at Riverside, kind of like a homecoming. We got sillier and sillier until we just couldn't work on our projects anymore. I'm sure the therapist on duty thought our doctor had been wise to have us in the hospital.

But, I was really glad to see that his defensive attitude was nearly gone; that's what gave me the most satisfaction. He showed this in subtle ways, one of which was smiling when he was asked for clarification, instead of frowning. He seemed more relaxed with people.

We spent Labor Day weekend in the hospital. The prospect of a long three-day weekend seemed glum indeed. On that Saturday evening when I had returned from a visit home, I was walking down the hall on the way to my room when a hand came out of the dayroom and grabbed my arm and pulled me in.

"Look!" Neil squealed delightedly, shoving some little boxes in my hands. "They let me rent three movies to watch this weekend!"

We both screamed and danced around like little kids while I looked at the choices he made.

Sometimes I had the impression that Neil was as surprised at himself as the rest of us were. I think he was finding out after 13 years that there was some fun and humor inside him —
And in the world, too.

8

I was sitting in the dayroom, looking through a tour-guide book of Southern California someone had left there. I was born and raised in the Los Angeles area, and seeing all the familiar sites and scenes made me despair. I hadn't seen anyone in my own immediate family for nearly a year and a half, and as far as I knew, they didn't even know I was in the hospital. I was feeling as if the whole world was going merrily on without me while I was rotting away in a hospital that I had little hope of getting out of.

I was about to throw the book down in disgust when Neil literally ran in. He was breathing hard through his mouth, his nostrils were flared, and his eyes were darting back and forth in obvious fear.

"Those Portland police have a lot of nerve!" he gasped, looking back at the doorway into the hall.

I looked at the doorway, too, half expecting to see a police officer rush in, handcuffs in one hand and gun in the other.

I looked back at Neil and asked him what happened, but his only response was pacing around and gasping for air. I could see sweat glistening off the back of his neck.

"Neil! What happened?!" I repeated, fear knotting my stomach when he didn't answer at once.

"I was in the bank," he began, pacing in front of me, still eyeing the doorway, "and there was this cop in front of me in line, and he wanted the financial records of somebody, but the teller wouldn't give it to him, because he didn't have a court order. He gave her a real hassle, so she told him to see this other lady, but the other lady wouldn't give them to him, either. I heard her say, 'No sir, not without a court order!'"

He stopped to get his breath.

"So, did he leave?" I asked, hoping Neil hadn't been drawn into an ugly scene.

"Yeah, I asked the teller if he'd wanted my records, but she said he didn't. But, I'm not so sure if they'd tell me the truth."

"Oh, Neil," I said, collapsing back on the couch in relief, "why would they want your records? Do you have anything to hide?"

"No, but he could have seen me go in the bank and decided he wanted them and then ..."

"Wasn't the policeman at the bank before you got there?" I interrupted. "Wouldn't it be really coincidental that he'd want your records at the precise time you happened to be in the bank?"

Neil sat down on the couch next to me in thought, worry wrinkles all over his forehead. "Yeah ... but he could have recognized me and decided he wanted my hospital records."

I closed my eyes in disbelief. I couldn't believe he could make so much of such a trivial incident.

Finally, opening my eyes, I touched him on the arm. "Neil," I said, softly, "I signed a form when I was admitted that said nobody could have access to my hospital records unless I gave permission. Did you sign that form?"

After a moment of thought, he said, "Yeah, but they could get a court order and ..."

"So what?" I said in exasperation. "What are they going to see? You've been straight here. They can't drag you out and lock you up. They'd probably have to go through Dr. Larsen to do that, anyway."

I paused to look at him. He had calmed down and was just looking at the floor, his face a study.

"If you don't have anything to hide, you probably don't have anything to fear," I finished up, hoping I was allaying his fears.

The face that looked up at me was so sad. I wanted to put my arms around him and tell him everything would be okay, like I would do for my little son.

"It's just that they can do it, you know? It's just that they can get a court order and make it hell for me."

I swallowed a lump in my throat. "I know," I said softly, rubbing his shoulder. "I know."

As I watched him leave a few minutes later, I thought somberly to myself: Neil is such a little boy — a little boy afraid of cracks in the ceiling and monsters in the closet. Such a sad and scared little boy.

9

Often, while I was in the hospital, seeing all the sad faces and tragic situations made me wish everyone knew God. No one mentioned God, so I simply assumed no one believed He existed. No wonder they can't cope, I'd say to myself. They don't know of a Power greater than themselves to draw on, to rely on.

But I didn't know how to share that resource. For one thing, I felt it would be so trite to approach anybody there with a "You need God," because everyone was so much worse off than I was. It could easily be interpreted as being awfully simplistic.

Also, I felt like it would be the height of hypocrisy. From where I stood, God was paying too much attention to the sparrows. A great deal of the time I felt like I was in a dark pit, futily trying to claw my way out, forgotten by God. I couldn't even pray for myself.

At the beginning of my depression, I had discovered Psalm 139, and I clung to that message, referring to it several times a day.

A good friend of mine wrote a note to me saying we didn't have to have faith in our faith, but to just have faith in God. She told me that even though I didn't feel it, God loved me, she loved me, and everyone was praying for me. I kept that note by my bedside, and it became dog-eared from my constant reading.

At one point, Logan reminded me that the Holy Spirit intercedes for us; that I didn't have to form words to pray to God. So, I just started sending feelings His way — black, desperate, and frustrated feelings.

These things comforted me somewhat, but how could I share God with these poor, needy people when I couldn't see God working in <u>my</u> situation at all?

An answer came one day when I was eating lunch with Neil and Bob. We were talking about relaxation techniques when Neil said, "I'll bet Jesus Christ didn't need any relaxation techniques; He was always relaxed."

My mouth dropped open in surprise. "Oh no, Neil," I said, as much in surprise at what he said as by the fact that he mentioned Jesus Christ. "The night He was betrayed, He sweat drops of blood — that's not relaxed."

"Doesn't it say somewhere that He was a man of sorrows and acquainted with grief?" Bob asked.

My mouth did a repeat performance of dropping open as I swung my head over to look at Bob. Apparently, the people here were less ignorant of religious matters than I thought. "Uh... yes," I managed to say at last. "... In Isaiah."

I turned back to Neil after Bob lapsed back into his customary silence. "And He had a lot of arguments with the Pharisees. That's not very relaxing. It eventually led to a kangaroo court where He was sentenced to death and crucified."

"Hmmm ..." Neil mused, chewing on a piece of roll. "I guess all the pictures I've ever seen of Him looked so peaceful, I thought He was pretty laid back all the time."

"Well, He said He had peace, but peace isn't the same thing as being relaxed. I guess part of His peace was that He knew why He was here — He was sure of His mission. That was the divine part of Him, I suppose."

I was about to elaborate on that, but Neil broke in. "I'm about half through reading John. That's like Jesus' biography, huh?"

"Yeah," I answered in amazement. "There are three other biographies, too, you know — Matthew, Mark, and Luke."

"Hmmm ..." Neil responded, taking a bite, thinking hard.

When he didn't say any more, I offered, "John is my favorite, though. He emphasizes love, and that appeals to me." After a pause, I added, "John wrote I, II, and III John, too. They're letters to people."

"Really?" Neil looked surprised, He took a bite of spaghetti. "Well ... I don't like Paul, you know? He sounds too full of himself. I'm just gonna believe what Jesus Christ Himself said, not some guy trying to reform people."

I smiled. "Yeah, Peter says somewhere in the Bible that Paul says some hard things. You're not alone in your opinion of Paul."

I didn't say anything more, mostly because I was afraid they'd think I was too preachy and "full of myself." Besides, I couldn't think of anything more to say.

Neil fixed me with the bug-under-the-microscope stare. After a few minutes he said, "You really know a lot about the Bible, don't you?"

I shrugged my shoulders, smiling ruefully. "Not as much as I'd like to; I study as often as I can. My relationship with God is very important to me."

Neil turned back to his meal, eyebrows down. I don't remember what we talked about after that, but I do remember hoping Neil would finish reading John.

10

"Oh, I know I'm paranoid," Neil was saying, "It's hard to get better, ya know? I feel like I've been crossed by everybody. I don't know who I can trust."

We were sitting on a park bench at Johnson Creek Park. It was beautiful there. Johnson Creek runs through the middle of the park, and I was watching the water swirl around the rocks. The late summer sun felt warm on our backs.

I was going through a rough time. My feelings had eclipsed. When I first entered the hospital, it was the only safe place for me. There was no way I could cope with being at home and all the responsibilities there. Now my medications were working so well that I wasn't depressed anymore — just extremely anxious and insecure about how my body reacted to stress. Also, when I first entered the hospital, I was comforted to see all the patients so much worse off than I was; I wasn't so bad off after all. But now, their problems were weighing heavily on me. Everywhere I turned I saw pain, and it was getting to me.

Yet, when I was home, it seemed to me that though I saw everything familiar, nothing was the same. I'd wander around the house, looking for me, and I'd always leave with the frightening feeling that the old me was gone forever.

"It's awful, Neil," I had said as we walked, on our way to the park. "I don't want to be in the hospital anymore, and I don't want to go home, either."

He had convinced me, rather against my will, to come for this walk. I told him I was just too tired and not in the mood, but he went into one of his Dr. Larsen impersonations: "Regular exercise will reduce the stress level in your body, give you more energy, and increase the chemicals in your brain that cause a feeling of well-being."

His Dr. Larsen gestures were perfect. I had to laugh. Probably half the patients on the East Unit were Dr. Larsen's patients, and we entertained each other with Dr. Larsen impersonations.

"Yeah," he responded to my statement of frustration. "That's kind of how I feel, except there's really nowhere else for me to go right now."

When we got to the park, we talked awhile about how we'd both grown since we'd been at Riverside. That's when he started talking about being paranoid. I asked him if he trusted Dr. Larsen.

"Oh yeah," Neil said, definitely. "He's the best; I can't believe how lucky I am to finally get some help. And I've been in and out of hospitals, and Riverside is the best I've been in." He paused to light a cigarette. "I just wish I could get it together faster and get on with my life. After 13 years of drifting around, I'd like to be doing something productive."

I asked him if he'd been depressed before Vietnam. He thought about it, taking a drag on his cigarette.

"Oh, I was a little, you know, when I was going to school. I didn't want to go full-time, because I didn't know what I wanted to major in. But, I knew if I didn't go full-time, I'd get drafted." He took a deep breath, looking straight ahead. "There was a lot of pressure."

He looked past me at some children playing on the swings. "My dad was in the F.B.I., and he wanted me to enlist." He laughed bitterly. "He was a real right-winger and pro-war. I felt confused. My guts told me that the war was wrong, you know? And I didn't want any part of it. Besides, I didn't want anything interfering with my life like that."

He took a deep breath again and looked at the ground. "It was the first time I realized my dad wasn't God, you know?"

Neil had been really stingy about details about his family. He had mentioned the week before three brothers and three sisters, and when I commented on what a large family that was, he had shrugged his shoulders and said matter-of-factly, "I come from a Catholic family; what can I say?"

"Is your dad still in the F.B.I.?" I was asking him now.

"No, he teaches criminology," he answered.

"Where does your family live?"

"My folks live in North Carolina, and some of the rest of them live in Virginia."

"Were you born in North Carolina?"

He looked up, his eyes wide, his expression defensive. "No, I was born in New York!" (His whole manner had changed) —
Like he was challenging me in some way.

"Oh," I said, trying to appear nonchalant. "That's interesting."

I watched him for a minute. "Did you grow up in New York?"

He shrugged impatiently. "No, my parents just happened to be in New York at the time. I grew up in Virginia." Then he changed the subject. "I think I'd like to go back to school to ... uh ... maybe be a teacher or a coach."

"I think you'd make a great teacher!" I said, enthusiastically. I remembered how patient he'd been with Pattie. I was also remembering how he lectured Florence and me on the weights in the recreation room in the basement of the hospital. He knew what exercises strengthened which muscles. I had surprised him by easily picking up a 20-pound barbell.
If there is anything in shape on a mother with a young child, it's her arms.

"Yeah ... well ... I thought about being a lawyer, but if I have a police record, that's out." He got up and started pacing about.

I watched the creek in silence. I was thinking about Leighton. The last time I saw him, his pants were too short. I wondered if Logan knew where his Size 4 clothes were. I wondered if I would ever get to a place where I could enjoy caring for my sweet son again.

"It must be nice being married to the right person," Neil said, sitting down again.

I smiled down at our feet. "Yeah, it really is. I haven't been able to enjoy it much lately, but it is a real blessing to always have somebody to love and somebody to love you back."

Neil was looking at our feet, too. "Maybe someday I'll have that, too. But it's a hard thing to picture."

He ran his fingers through his hair. "I've just got too many things on my mind right now."

He jumped up suddenly and asked if I was ready to go. Without waiting for an answer, he strode on ahead without me. I wearily pulled myself off the bench and started off after him.

What happened between you and your family, Neil? I wondered to myself. What happened that would make you so reluctant to talk about them? What happened in Vietnam?

It suddenly dawned on me as I caught up with him that there was so little I knew about the person walking beside me. In some ways he was an open book, and in other ways an impenetrable vault.

11

Neil and I had several such talks and walks, and though it seems as if we spent a lot of time together, there were whole days when all I saw of him was a brief hello in the hall or a wave in the cafeteria.

Neil was more involved in hospital activities than I was. His counseling schedule was heavier and he was assigned to biofeedback. He also had a lot of writing to do connected with his therapy. Every morning there was a physical education group, and Neil rarely missed it. He often tried to pull me into this activity, but if I came at all, I just watched. I've always been reticent about playing sports, and most of the time I felt too dizzy to play, anyway. Even though I encouraged him to come to group therapy, he never came after that one painful session.

I busied myself with relaxation tapes, interacting with other patients, and outings with my family. I also often needed a lot of time alone to pull myself together.

This is why I'm not really sure when Kathy entered Neil's life. My first indication was when we were watching a movie in the dayroom one evening. Kathy came in half-way through the movie. She sat down next to Neil and asked him what the plot was. He no sooner got started than she started crying about something. She made such a scene that he finally led her to a far corner of the room, pulled over two chairs, and sat down with her. They were still talking when I left after the movie was over.

As time went by I saw them spending more and more time together. At first I marveled that he could put up with the constant chatter. He didn't seem to mind it much, though there were a couple of times I saw him make a hasty exit when she came into a room.

When I overheard her telling him that she'd leave some prayers on his pillow to comfort him, I despaired. She had offended several people with her pushy evangelism, and I felt she was the type of person that made religion repulsive to some people and ludicrous to others. I didn't want Neil to think Kathy's idea of religion was all there was.

One night I saw him explaining to her how to use dental floss. I couldn't believe it — dental floss! My three-year-old knows how to use dental floss! But, he had the same patience and kindness with Kathy that I'd seen him display with Pattie and Letha ... and with me. I watched him, and I thought: Neil, you're such a good person, and you don't even know it.

I had the opportunity to tell him not long afterwards in a morning community meeting. Roger (the Hun) thought it would be a good idea to start out the morning by giving each other some good strokes, so we were to tell the person on our left something we liked about him or her. Neil was on my left.

When it came to my turn, Neil was hunched over double, looking at his feet, his back to me. He looked like I was going to use a whip on him.

"Ah, Neil," I began, taking pleasure in putting my feelings into words, "Neil is one of those genuinely good people. He's kind and patient and gentle. I enjoy his company very much, and my stay here wouldn't be nearly as valuable to me without Neil."

When I finished, he slowly looked up, amazement written all over his face. There was silence for several seconds. "Uh ... that was real nice of you to say those things ..."

"They were easy to say, Neil."

"Well, uh ... thanks."

"You're welcome,"

The bug-under-the-microscope look came, and he looked that way until Roger reminded him that it was his turn to praise Alan who was on Neil's left.

I had another opportunity to let him know how I felt while we were in Arts and Crafts several days later. Neil was never afraid to ask questions, no matter how silly. He always wanted to get things right. I, on the other hand, was often afraid to ask for fear of appearing dumb.

"You know what I admire about you, Neil?" I asked him as he worked on his key chains and I worked on my embroidery.

Haunted eyes met mine. There was a pause. "What?" he asked cautiously.

I smiled.   "You're a real survivor."

He started laughing. "Yeah, well, that's about all you can say for me."

"No!" I protested. "You have a lot of good qualities. Even after all these years of hurt, you still set yourself up for rejection over and over by asking questions and seeking help time after time after time. That's a rare quality, Neil."

We worked in silence for a while. Then he said thoughtfully, painting a coat of varnish on the leather, "Yeah, even when I had my nervous breakdown, my spirit was in there fighting." He stopped painting and looked at me. "And you know what? You really care about people, even when there's nothing in it for you. That's a rare quality, too."

I smiled, my turn to be surprised. I guess turnabout is fair play, because if I surprised him, he certainly surprised me time after time. Several times he commented on how calm I was. Me! The panic attack queen of the world!

I remember one incident when I was waiting for Shelli to get me a Xanax. I was concentrating on holding my insides together, because surely they would fly apart if I didn't have something to calm me quickly. Shelli seemed to be taking her time about getting it, which added to my tension.

Neil waltzed by, touched me lightly on the arm and said, "There's Miss Relaxation, looking calm as usual."

This wasn't the first time he had mentioned my "calm;" otherwise I would have thought he was joking. I couldn't even answer. I was sure I was a picture of a nervous breakdown waiting to happen.

When I looked up at him, he was studying me. And I thought to myself: What kind of eyes are you looking at me with? You are so blind!

12

Mary and I were eating lunch together; or rather, she was eating and I was looking at my food, my stomach turning. I hadn't slept well the night before and was deciding to skip Arts and Crafts after lunch in favor of a nap. Neil came over with his tray, banged it down next to Mary, across the table from me, sat down heavily, and started eating, glowering the whole time.

I hadn't talked to Neil in a couple of days. I remember thinking dully that something must be wrong, but it was Mary who asked the question.

"What's up?" she asked.

"I got a call from my lawyer!" he said, spitting the word "lawyer" out like a wad of chewing tobacco.

I watched him for a minute with weary eyes. "And?" I finally asked.

"<u>And</u> she told me the judge wants to see me all by myself if I want to switch lawyers. I can't <u>do</u> that! It's illegal. I can't go before a judge without proper representation! It's a trap! They'll get me down there and they'll ..."

"Neil" I broke in, "Have you told Dr. Larsen? Maybe he'll go with you."

"Yeah, I told him. And he says he'll go with me, but he wants me to act all contrite and say I was wrong because I was sick, and he'll write a letter to document it. Well, it makes me sick to think about it. I <u>wasn't</u> wrong! It's this damn corrupt justice system! They're trying to nail me!" He jabbed his roast beef with his fork.

"Neil," Mary said, calmly, leaning over to him. "I just imagine Dr. Larsen wants you to play their little game and that way you'll get off the hook. That's what you want, isn't it?"

"Yeah, well, I'm not going to do it!" he responded vehemently. "This thing isn't going to be over 'til I'm dead and in my grave. This isn't going to blow over 'til I'm dead and in my grave! They're not going to have any peace 'til I'm dead and in my grave!"

He was getting more worked up with every sentence, and I wanted to get off the subject of death and graves, so I broke in, smiling weakly, "Well ... you'll certainly go down swinging."

"No!" he blared, eyes blazing. "I'm not going down! I'm gonna be like Jesus Christ — if you're my friend, great. If not, you'll wish you were never born!"

I listened in dismay. Oh, Neil, I thought, I hope you finish reading John. Jesus had nothing but love for his enemies.

Neil was still ranting. "I'm not going down without bringing all of them with me!"

I had to leave. I could feel the hate reaching out and scorching me.

13

When I came into the cafeteria that evening, Neil was sitting by himself. I had taken my nap, but I was still weary. I felt as if I had wrestled all afternoon and was no closer to a solution about my future. The hospital was becoming unbearable, yet I knew if I went home, I'd probably end up in the hospital again in short order. I felt trapped with no hope of escape.

I saw that Neil had finished his meal and was smoking a cigarette. He didn't appear very happy, but I figured if he didn't want company, he could leave without appearing rude after he finished his cigarette. So I sat down across from him.

I toyed with my food in silence, taking a bite now and then. Neil studied me. This went on for maybe five minutes.

I had just about decided I was through when Neil said, "Can't you take just one or two more bites? The more nourishment you get, the less tired you'll be." He was the one that sounded tired.

I can't," I said miserably. "My stomach is like a Venus fly trap. It's okay until I put something in it and then it just closes up so tight it hurts."

"You want me to get you a roast beef sandwich instead? That's a little lighter than that lasagna."

He was already on his feet, so I agreed. He was back before I put down my fork.

"Now, just think about something else while you chew ... like playing football, or something."

I stopped chewing to look at him incredulously. "Thanks, Neil," I said, dryly. "You'd make a great coach."

He snorted. "Yeah, well, that's out. I was talking to Anne this afternoon, and I told her I wanted to be a teacher or coach, and she said, 'Oh, no, Neil. That's not for you. It'll take at least six years, and you don't want to do that.'"

Anne was one of Neil's therapists. I was shocked and angry that she would be so negative. Apparently, Neil had had a rough day.

I decided to tell him about a conversation I had had with Dr. Larsen about a week earlier. I was distressed because one therapist would tell me one thing and another would tell me something else, and I didn't agree with either of them. He told me that everyone ultimately has to decide for himself what is right for him and go with it. He said to just take the good things and throw out what I couldn't use.

"It's hard," I ended up, "because I feel so vulnerable here. It's hard to know who is on target about me and who has missed me completely."

"Yeah ... I don't know, either," Neil said slowly, worry lines all over his forehead. I hated seeing that pained expression; I wanted to take my hand and smooth his forehead 'til it was perfectly smooth.

"Well, I think you'd be a good teacher," I said, trying to be positive, hoping to make him feel better. "Yeah, but six years! That's a long time."

"So what? You'd be doing something productive. You'd be working on something you'd want to do."

He sighed in response. "Barbara told me last night I should prepare myself for failure in suing the government. She said I had little chance of succeeding and I should just think about getting better and get on with my life. But, I <u>can't</u> think of failing, don't you see?"

No, I didn't see, but I wasn't going to tell him that. He ran his hand over his eyes while I watched helplessly, wishing I could say something that would help.

"People don't understand the magnitude of my problem. My mom told me that this doctor gave her some glasses that gave her headaches for a year because they were the wrong prescription. She told me, 'Doctors make mistakes sometimes. You just got to pick yourself up and go on.'" He threw his hands in the air. "She was comparing that to my nervous breakdown. That made me mad for a long time."

I looked out the window at the building next door. I could see a plant hanging from a macramé hanger. I thought about my plants at home, probably dying from neglect.

Finally, I said, "It's harder, I think, when you grow up a compliant child. I was always avoiding a fight, doing what other people told me to do, eager to please. But when you become an adult, you have to go with your own instincts about what is best for you, because there are a lot of mixed messages in the world, and you go crazy trying to please everybody."

Neil ground out his cigarette in the ashtray. "Yeah, I was a compliant child, too. But, I've changed. Nobody's telling <u>me</u> how to live my life."

I looked at his furrowed brow, his haunted eyes, his sad mouth. I thought about how he scrupulously followed the rules at Riverside, his impeccable manners, his drive to do things exactly right. I thought of his doubts about a career choice because of Anne. And I thought: No, Neil, you're still that compliant little boy — a little more bravado, perhaps — but you're still Mrs. McCarthy's compliant little boy, eager to please.

14

The community meeting had barely begun when we heard a frantic voice call over the P.A. system. "Code 4! Code 4! All available therapists to West Unit, please! Code 4!"

Both the tone of the voice and the look on Roger's face as he jumped from his chair made my blood run cold and the hair on the back of my neck stand on end.

"We'll get together later!" Roger yelled as he shot out the door.

We all sat, stunned. Somebody asked what that was all about. Mary stood up with a disgusted, bored sigh. "It's just some goon over on West Unit that's gone berserk — that's all. They need everybody to hold him down while they knock him out with a shot." She started out the door. "Wonder who it is this time." She stifled a yawn.

I sat frozen to my chair, certain that if there had been anything in my stomach at the beginning of the meeting, it would be making its way out now. I began wondering if I was working on an ulcer.

I felt something soft on my wrist. It was Neil's hand, gently pulling me to my feet. "Let's get outta here," he whispered.

Numbly, I allowed him to pull me out the door. As he signed us out, I looked at my hands, my feet, the ceiling, the walls, trying to block out all the scenarios my imagination was creating about what was taking place on the other side of the hospital. I looked at Neil. His dark features looked as if they had turned to stone.

By the time we hit the sidewalk outside, tears were silently making their way down my cheeks. It was cloudy, and I thought to myself: This day is me — cloudy and gray. Oh, God, did I die without knowing it and end up in hell? This is truly madness. I'm afraid I'll never be normal again if I don't get away from all this. I feel so cornered, so lost, so scared!

We walked for several blocks without speaking, each of us wrapped up in our own thoughts. I was just acknowledging a headache starting and wishing I could go to bed and wake up in about five years when Neil asked me if I knew of any hiking trails nearby.

"Wh-what?" I sniffed, trying without much success to change gears in my mind.

"Dr. Larsen said I could get a six-hour pass some weekend to go hiking, and I was wondering where I could go. Somebody said you could hike over by the zoo. Have you ever been there?"

I stared at him, bewildered. His recovery from the scene we had just left was, to me, remarkable. The wind had picked up, and I noticed Neil's dark hair blowing straight out on one side, like a clown's. My own hair was blowing around and sticking to my wet face. I suddenly remembered part of a scripture: *"Forgetting what is behind and straining toward what is ahead..."(Phil. 3:13)* Then I realized Neil's eyes were staring back at mine, waiting for an answer.

"Uh ... Washington Park ... yeah," I said, wiping the hair away from my face, still trying to plug into the subject of conversation. "But not to hike ... uh ... I hear that there are some nice trails, though. It's beautiful there."

"Do you like to hike" he asked me, kicking a rock along the sidewalk like a little kid, making me smile.

"I don't know," I answered. "I've never hiked before."

"Ah," he said, jumping in the gutter after the rock and kicking it back on the sidewalk.

No more was said about hiking, and we started taking turns kicking the rock back to the hospital. I studied Neil as we ran around each other after the ever-moving piece of stone.

I'd like to be like Neil someday, I thought. Someday I'd like to be able to let go of the things I can't do anything about. I'd like to stop over-reacting. I'd like to feel sad about bad times for just a little while and then just get on with my life and kick a rock home.

15

A turning point in the eclipse of my feelings came the next day. And I think a turning point came for Neil, too.

Mary was reaching some kind of crisis in her problem, the details of which were never made known to me. Her doctor confined her to the hospital; she was allowed no passes outside. Since her usual reaction to stress was to escape to a friend's house for a couple of hours, or going home, or just going for a drive, this was excruciating for her.

The tension in our room rose sharply. That day I lived from Xanax to Xanax. I couldn't think clearly, and I had an overwhelming feeling of dread.

The situation finally reached a climax that evening in the cafeteria. Mary started shouting at Marvin, providing a generally ugly scene. As I watched in horror a panic attack suddenly overwhelmed me.

I grabbed my tray, threw it in the general direction of the dirty dish table and ran to the East Unit. Shelli took one look at me and barked, "Xanax, right?"

As soon as I gulped it down, I ran out the door and into the evening air. But I didn't notice it; I didn't even know where I was going.

Logan drove up about then, and I vaulted into the cab of the truck. For a long while I sobbed on his chest.

"I want to go home," I heard myself saying, "I want to go home." And all of a sudden, I knew I meant it.

I thought of reading to Leighton and doing dishes and going to baby showers and seeing friends. And suddenly I wanted to do all those ordinary things. A light came on in my mind that I <u>wanted</u> to deal with the logical reality of the outside world. The hospital's reality was the warped quality of Alice in Wonderland.

I knew, even as I wept, that my panic attack would end — I wouldn't die — nothing awful would happen. It would just end. It did, and I wasn't afraid of having one anymore.

An hour and a half later I walked (and I use that term loosely) on the East Unit, feeling drained and very, very tired. I had a headache from crying so long, and my hair was whipped all over my head — it had been a windy evening. I must have looked a sight.

Neil was just coming out of his room as I staggered slowly by. He stopped mid-stride and gaped at me. He was wearing shorts — he must have just finished working out in the weight room.

This little voice came out of my throat as I went by, "Hi, Neil." I was surprised I was still capable of speaking.

"Uh ... hi ... uh ..." he stammered after me.

When I got to the nurse's station to ask for a Tylenol, Shelli pulled me behind the counter and asked me what "the hell" was wrong.

I choked out what had happened in the cafeteria. Barbara, who was Mary's therapist for the evening, suggested a change of room for me. Shelli agreed since

Mary's doctor had mentioned that she may need to have a private room soon.

"In the meantime," Barbara said, taking me by the shoulders and propelling me down the hall, "why don't you come to a communications class that's starting as soon as I can round up some people?"

I just wanted to fall down where I was and roll into an inert ball, but I had no initiative to resist. I was clutching the Styrofoam cup filled with water I had used to take the Tylenol with, and some crackers Shelli had given me, so I wouldn't be taking the Tylenol on an empty stomach. Barbara led me into a classroom.

I was the first one there. I sat in the chair nearest the door, marveling that my body wasn't melting all over the chair and onto the floor. Like a shock victim, I was nibbling my cracker and staring ahead of me when Neil came in.

He stopped in front of me for a second, paced around for a bit, then finally sat down next to me. I couldn't speak to him; I couldn't even look at him. I was afraid I'd burst into hysterical crying. I just stared at the floor and sipped my water.

"Uh ... you've got really nice shoes on tonight," he said, smiling up into my downcast face.

I looked at my four-year-old J.C. Penney, blue and white jogging shoes that I'd worn every day since entering the hospital and then looked back at Neil, suppressing a giggle. Somehow, his comment unleashed the conviction that though I had been going through a rough time, I was still among friends.

I hope my face smiled back at him. "Thanks, Neil," I choked out.

He jerked his head in the direction of my shoes. "They look like little football shoes."

Now I was laughing out loud and feeling much better. In fact, I wanted to grab him and hug him, but I was afraid it would be misinterpreted.

Others were coming into the room, and Barbara gave a little speech on communication and listening, most of which I'd heard before in college and in seminars.

We did a little exercise that involved pairing up for thirty seconds; one partner would tell the other some things about himself. Then the next thirty seconds the process was reversed. When that was over, we reported to the group what we had learned about the other.

"I don't know what to say!" Neil whispered to me, panicky.

"Okay," I said. "I'll go first."

I told him about my family, where I was born, how old I was, and that I had a Bachelor's degree. By then, my turn was over.

Now it was Neil's turn. "Uh ... I was born in Brooklyn, New York on August 29, 1950. I ... uh ... was raised in Charlottesville, Virginia. I don't like science or trigonometry ... oh ... uh ... I like playing and watching sports ... uh ... I don't know what else to say!"

By this time, mercifully, his thirty seconds was up. We talked about how intensely we had had to listen, eye contact, shutting out noises, etc.

Then Barbara asked for a volunteer.

When Neil volunteered, I think I heard the sound of everyone in the room gasping. Cautious, paranoid Neil had never volunteered for anything without knowing exactly what was involved, and even then it was with reluctance.

"Okay, Neil," Barbara said. "We're going to send you out of the room, set up an obstacle course, and Judy is going to lead you back to your seat by verbally giving you directions.

I gulped. Oh Lord, why me?

When Neil came back into the room, blindfolded, he started waving his arms around him wildly, trying to get his bearings.

"No, Neil," Barbara said. "Keep your hands at your sides and let Judy give you all the information."

I felt all the pressure of an air-traffic controller, talking down a plane being flown by a child.

"Okay, Neil," I started. "Let's go real slow. Take little steps until I tell you to stop."

His steps were so mincing that I thought we'd be there all night before he got half-way across the room, so I told him he'd be all right if his steps were normal, but slow.

"You're doing great, Neil. Now, take three steps more ... Okay, good. Now turn slightly to your left ... a little more ... okay, great! Take two steps ... okay, one more. Good, you're doing fine, Neil." I could see beads of sweat all over his face. My heart was running a marathon inside my chest, my hands wringing.

"Now, make a right angle to your right. Great! You can go about five steps ... okay ... one step more. Good! Now make a right angle turn again ... oh, Neil, I'm sorry. I made a mistake. Make a right angle turn, but to your left this time. Good!" I could see the sweat raining off his face onto his shirt.

"Okay, take two more steps ... one more ... one more ... okay! You're in front of your chair!"

The whole room erupted in cheers. Neil flopped into his chair, and when he took off his blindfold, I grabbed his wrist and shouted above the din. "You did it, Neil! You did it!" I was ecstatic that he'd gone out on a limb in trust and was so successful.

The face that looked up at me was one I had never seen before. I had always thought Neil was good looking. When he smiled, it was usually with just one side of his mouth, and it was usually a rueful or half-hearted smile. But this time, his whole mouth was smiling wide at me; I could see his teeth. I discovered he had dimples! And his eyes — his eyes were full of joy without a trace of pain. His whole face, sweaty as it was, was radiant. It was obvious to me that he had forgotten for a moment all the struggles he was dealing with.

And I thought to myself: You are so handsome, Neil! I could see in one instant all the potential for a normal life that Neil had.

I wanted to freeze that moment in time forever.

16

That night, alone in my new room, I reveled in the calm, the absolute absence of tension. And I made an important decision.

That morning, Dr. Larsen had ordered progesterone, the hormone in which I was deficient, to be taken twice a day in suppository form. It had just been made available in Portland and had made a dramatic positive difference in other PMS patients. That was the hope for me, and I had just taken my first dosage.

This was Thursday evening. I would tell Dr. Larsen in the morning that I wanted to go home for several hours on both Saturday and Sunday; and if I felt good at home, I wanted to be discharged on Monday morning.

That decision made, I went to sleep and slept better than I had in a long time. I wanted to go home, and I was on my way.

The next morning, I woke up feeling great. I danced into the doctor's room behind the nurse's station, proposed my plans, and Dr. Larsen enthusiastically agreed.

I'll always remember that last weekend as, for the most part, jolly and happy. I felt like celebrating.

I told Neil that night as we were watching a football game together.

"Monday?" he asked, sitting up suddenly. "This Monday?"

"Yeah! I'm kind of scared, but I feel so good I just don't feel like I belong here anymore. At first, I really needed the hospital, and now I feel like I need to go home."

"Yeah ... I ... uh ... kind of feel that way, too. I mean, what's left for me here now? The therapists are just saying the same old things, and my meds are all stabilized."

While he lit a cigarette, I asked him what he was going to do when he got out of the hospital.

"I think I'll just go to Astoria and maybe live with Marvin. Dr. Larsen said he can refer me to a doctor there, and there's a community college there, too, in case I want to go back to school."

He adjusted himself on the couch to face me. "They've got a chess club, Marvin says. And if it all falls apart for me, Astoria's close enough that I can get back here for help. I've just got to get out of Portland — too many bad memories, you know?"

"You'd come back, Neil?" I asked. "I mean, if you needed help again? For sure?"

"Oh, yeah," he said, positively. "This place and Larsen pulled me out of a pit."

He talked on about how he liked to hike and camp and about the gear he'd have to have to keep out the rain. Astoria, he felt, was a big enough town that there'd be plenty to do there, yet small enough that he wouldn't need a car to get around. We talked about the Oregon coast, and I told him of our vacation in Lincoln City the previous May.

"I should write my sister after I have an address in Astoria so she'll ship me the stuff I left with her. I've got a real nice stereo system." He ran his hands through his hair. "It'll probably take her a couple of years."

"Where does your sister live?" I asked.

"Oh, she lives in Virginia."

"Why would it take her, a couple of years?"

He shrugged. "She's got a couple of kids, and she's pretty out of it a lot of the time. It takes her a long time to get things done. She put it in a closet; she may have gotten rid of it by now."

I was horrified. "Why would she have gotten rid of it?"

He shrugged again, "I don't know. I haven't been in contact with her for a couple of years. She might have just got tired of having it around."

A touchdown was made, and Neil went back to watching football for a few minutes.

"Marvin says there are lots of camping places and hiking trails around Astoria," Neil began again, after watching them make the extra point. "What I'd really like to do is hike all up and down the Oregon coast."

"Well," I said, stretching, "you certainly sound like you've thought this all out."

"Yeah, I'm anxious to get on with things. I've been thinking about what to do with myself for a long time, and this is the first time I feel like it might work."

As we watched the rest of the game, I remember feeling so glad for Neil. It was good to see him so optimistic.

17

There was one incident which marred that last weekend, maybe because I didn't understand it and still don't. It has come to haunt me.

Logan and I had planned for me to come home for six hours — my longest time since being in the hospital — on Saturday, and he was going to pick me up at 9:00.

I bounded out of bed at 8:00, hastily dressed, and ran to the cafeteria for breakfast. In my excitement, all I could manage was a glass of milk, and I carried it over to the table where Neil and Mary were eating.

As soon as I sat down, Mary left, saying she was waiting for a phone call from her doctor and had "things to do."

I had nearly finished my milk before Neil spoke. He told me of the conversation he and Mary had just had, reminiscing about how things had been a month ago. Now, most of the patients that had been in the hospital then were gone.

"And now you'll be gone," he finished up.

We went on talking and laughing and doing some remember-when's until I realized I was running late, so I excused myself, jumped up, and left.

I was leaning on the counter of the nurse's station a few minutes later, waiting for a multi-vitamin and some Xanax when Neil joined me.

He was leaning on the counter, too, and staring ahead. "Hey, you know, I've been thinking. Maybe you could just stay another week? Dr. Larsen said maybe I could get out at the end of next week. Then ... well ... you know, maybe we could get out about the same time."

I was feeling so chipper that I couldn't imagine staying in the hospital another week. In fact, I felt like I was biding my time staying the weekend. I assumed he knew how I felt, having explained it to him the night before, so I thought he was joking.

I laughed. "Neil, not even for you am I going to stay another week. I'm going to get out as soon as I can! And I can't wait!" My enthusiasm was boundless.

Neil's sober face turned toward mine, his eyes on the floor. There was a pause and then, "Ah ... okay." Moving slowly, he started walking down the hall in the direction of his room.

I stared after him, perplexed. Could he be serious? We hadn't seen that much of each other since Kathy appeared on the scene; and besides, we had both been so busy. Even if I stayed, what good would it do? We'd still be going our separate ways after our discharges. Too late, I realized he wasn't joking.

"Neil!" I called after him and ran down the hall toward him.

He stopped but didn't turn around. I ran around him and faced him.

"I <u>have</u> to go home!" I said, beseeching him to understand. I made sweeping motions with my hands.

"I'm tired of all this. Everywhere I look is pain, and I can't stand it anymore. I'm tired of depending on someone else to give me my meds and let me off the unit because it's locked all the time, and I'm tired of the food and having to sign out. I miss my family, and they miss me. I just need to be home."

I looked into his eyes, hoping to read some understanding, but they were haunted, as usual, the rest of his face expressionless. Finally, he shut his eyes and nodded; then without a word went into his room.

I stared at his closed door in dismay. What did all this mean? What difference to him would one more week in the hospital make? I felt that somewhere I had really bungled something, but I didn't know what; that puzzle piece of understanding was missing.

I wanted to smash my fist through the wall.

18

That evening after dinner I went outside and sat down on a low cement wall that bordered the flower beds surrounding the hospital. Dr. Larsen's office was right around the corner.

I loved being home that day. I knew it was going to be rough getting back to a workable routine, and I was scared about being on my own again. But the hospital was representing more and more a prison of pain to me. It seemed a nuisance to come back that afternoon, and I didn't even want to stay inside any longer than I had to. So I was outside, watching ordinary people drive by and ordinary people call to their children. It would be good to be ordinary again.

I was also thinking about dinner. I had sat at the same table with Kathy; I didn't see Neil. She told Marvin and me what a great time she and Neil had had that day hiking near Washington Park. She was telling all of us that she and Neil were going to start dating after they got out of the hospital. I was surprised and then amused. I wondered how Neil felt about her. He was always very polite with her and went with her places and didn't seem to mind when she banged on his door late at night or hung on his arm. He hadn't talked to me about her, and I never brought her up; I didn't think it was any of my business.

I was thinking about all those things when Neil found me there. Sitting down next to me, he asked me how my day went. I was a little hesitant to tell him at first, considering our conversation that morning. But he was at ease and seemed happy and acted as if it had never taken place. Indeed, I began to wonder if I had imagined it.

He told me enthusiastically of his day of hiking. "I think maybe next weekend I'll go by myself and hike further. God, it felt good to stretch my legs!"

We went on chatting about our various plans after leaving the hospital. We talked about optimism.

"I've got these tapes in my mind, you know?" he said, tapping his forehead. "And they've told me for thirteen years that I can't do stuff and that nothing will turn out right. And I worry a lot. But, I'm changing those tapes. I'm changing those tapes so I can succeed and get better. I don't want to worry anymore. I want to use that energy to get better."

I smiled at him. "I've got a few tapes of my own to re-write."

Our hope for the future dominated our discussion. We talked the sun down. I smile even now as I remember it.

Ah, we were such comrades in recuperation that evening.

19

Kathy was chattering to Neil the next morning when I sat down with them for breakfast.

"Mom says you can sleep in my bed, and I'll sleep on the couch. She trusts you. She trusts me, too."

She turned to me and said proudly, "Neil is coming over to my mom's house next weekend for Mikey's birthday party! Isn't that wonderful?"

I looked at Neil. He didn't look up; he was busily devouring a bowl of oatmeal.

I smiled at Kathy. "That sounds like fun."

"And Neil is going to spend the night and everything, because my mom trusts Neil. I've already told him we can hold hands and hug, but no kissing for two years."

My cup of milk stopped half-way to my mouth. I looked at Neil again; he still didn't look up, but he was eating faster. I looked back at Kathy, my mouth open to say words, if only my brain would send the message of what to say.

Finally, I choked out, "Two years?"

"Judy," Kathy said earnestly, grabbing my arm, "I have high moral principles! I just can't be that intimate so soon. It isn't right."

"But two years?" was all I could say.

"There's just too many strong feelings to get when you're not married when you kiss. I have high moral principles!"

The words "two years" seemed to be bouncing off my skull, but coming back again and again like a boomerang. I'm sure I was gaping.

"Kathy," I managed to say, removing her hand from my arm, "I consider myself to have high moral principles, too. But, I never set a time limit on affection, certainly not two years!"

"Judy," she said, grabbing my arm again, "I can't be that serious so soon after what Gary has done to me! He kept telling me I didn't understand men. He was so cruel!"

I scratched my head with the hand that was connected to the arm she kept grabbing, which disentangled her from me. I could certainly see why Gary thought she didn't understand men.

"What about Hank?" I asked her. "Have you let him kiss you?"

"Oh, no!" she exclaimed, horrified. "We've only gone together a month and a half."

"Hmmm ..." I looked over at Neil. During this whole interchange, he had finished up his oatmeal and was half-way through his French toast. Not once had he looked up.

"But I know I can trust Neil. He's such a terrific guy." Kathy looked adoringly across the table at Neil.

I couldn't stand taking her seriously anymore. I couldn't let Neil get off so easily without at least a comment.

"Well, Neil," I said, suppressing a smile. "What do you think? Can you control yourself that long?"

He looked up and shrugged his shoulders. Grabbing his glass of juice, he said dryly, "Hey, what can I say? Hank's got seniority."

He gulped his juice down while Kathy and I laughed.

"Well, I have high moral principles," Kathy said again. "I don't think you should go all the way without being married." She was looking at me like I had told her to apply for a job as a topless dancer.

"Kathy," I said in frustration, "I don't think you should, either, but we're talking about two years for a kiss!"

To complicate matters, an older gentleman from the West Unit had sat down next to Neil. His name was Bob, and he had been admitted the day before. He didn't care if we were listening to him or if someone else was speaking; he interjected his comments whenever he felt like it.

"Sex is a glorious thing," said Bob.

"Okay," said Kathy, "Why do you think two years is too long?"

"How do you know how you'll be feeling in two years?" I countered. "How can you set a time for an activity that requires some feeling behind it?"

"I don't want to talk about it anymore," Kathy said. "You're all making fun of me."

"Love is important with sex," offered Bob.

"I'm sorry if you think I was making fun of you," I said. "I think it's admirable that you've set some values. I was just trying to understand them."

"Well, I don't want to talk about my values," she said, wiping her mouth with her napkin.

"Fine," I said. "Case closed."

"I just feel like I need to have high moral princi- ples, that's all," Kathy whined, turning to me.

I took a deep breath. "Kathy, you can still have high moral principles and kiss before two years," I said, struggling to keep my voice calm.

Bob stirred from his chair. "If you have sex with- out love, you're no better than a couple of hogs rooting around in the mud," he said loudly and stumbled off with his tray.

Neil and I looked around at the other patients whose attention had suddenly been drawn to our ta- ble. For a moment we sat, looking at each other and then burst into laughter. He pushed his hands against his thighs.

"For somebody who hates sex as much as you seem to, you sure do bring it up a lot," Neil said, shak- ing his head, obviously baffled.

Kathy was wiping her nose with a Kleenex. "You're all making fun of my high moral principles," she said plaintively.

I had reached my limit. I was not going to be sucked into this conversation any more. This had been the weirdest breakfast I had ever had.

"I'm sorry, Kathy," I said, getting up. "I wasn't making fun of you or your values. Excuse me."

As I walked out the cafeteria door, I thought that if I heard "high moral principles" one more time, I'd start screaming and then really belong in the hospital.

20

That evening I spent in my room — a sort of anti-climax to my last night in the hospital. I had thought about all kinds of pranks to pull to celebrate my discharge; but I refrained, fearful that they'd be misunderstood by the staff and my discharge jeopardized. The nurses and therapists had seen a lot of weird things, most of which were not pranks, so the mind-set was always to take the patient seriously.

I thought about dinner that evening. When I walked into the cafeteria, Neil raised his hand and yelled, "Hey, Judy, come over and join us." He and Marvin were alone at the table.

I smiled as I selected my food. Gone was the hesitant, cautious Neil. I didn't consider us bosom buddies — there was a vast gap of information about himself that Neil hadn't shared with me — but we had a comfortable relationship, and I felt good that he trusted me enough to yell across a room to seek my companionship.

When I was seated, Neil and Marvin eagerly told me of their day, as anxious to share their fun time as my son would be after being with his grandpa all morning.

While I had been on my outing at home, Marvin, Neil, and Kathy had gone out to lunch and then had bowled all afternoon. To my surprise, Marvin apparently had skunked the other two. Mild-mannered Marvin — there was a lot I didn't know about him, too.

Neil launched into an account of all the different kinds of bowling balls he used, never finding one to suit him. This set off some bantering between the two of them, Marvin teasing Neil about using the bowling balls as an excuse for losing.

"You should have seen Kathy," Marvin said. "Her score was 9."

I put my hand on my forehead. "9? Poor Kathy! Is she off in her room grieving about her poor showing?"

"No," Neil said. "She's seeing a pastor ... or somebody." There was silence for a few minutes while we ate.

"You know ..." Neil began, "Kathy embarrasses me sometimes."

I set down my fork. I was finished eating anyway, but the thought of Kathy made me angry, and my stomach tightened. There was something about her that defied logic. Sometimes, when it distressed me to see her simpering at Neil and acting "religious," I'd comfort myself by realizing that Neil needed to feel needed. I imagined that being with Kathy made him feel strong, and he needed that, too.

There was more silence as I watched him struggle to say the words that he wanted to use.

"I mean ..." he began again. "We go into a store and a clerk comes up and says, 'May I help you?' and Kathy will say, 'This is my friend, Neil, and we're not going to kiss for two years.' And the clerk will say, 'Oh, is there anything else I can do for you?"

Marvin and I laughed while Neil spread out his hands in exasperation. "It's embarrassing. I told her not to tell everybody that, but she does it anyway."

Neil took another bite. "I'm afraid it gives everybody the wrong idea. We're not ... lovers or anything — I'm not even romantically involved with her."

He sighed as he took another bite. "I just want us to be friends." He looked up at me, "you know? Kind of ... like ..." he waved a finger between him and me, "...us."

I smiled, touched. After a pause, I told him, "I don't think she sees it that way, Neil."

He rubbed his hand briefly over his forehead, and we went on talking of other things, lighter things, funny things. We laughed and joked until Neil left to spend the evening with his friend, Vaughn. I didn't see him again until the next morning.

I couldn't help thinking, as I sat in my room that last night in the hospital, that I'd played out that scene thousands of times before when I'd eaten in a college cafeteria, laughing and sharing.

Friends were still friends, even in a psychiatric hospital.

21

I woke up the next morning, my last morning in the hospital, to the sound of Dr. Larsen calling to one of his patients whose room was next door to mine. Although we normally saw him in the doctors' room behind the nurses' station, there were occasions when patients were too sick to make it that far. Apparently, Dr. Larsen was seeing her in her room.

Oh no! I thought to myself as I jumped up and started to put on my socks. One of my last thoughts as I fell asleep the night before was that I hoped I'd see the doctor first thing in the morning, so I'd be discharged as soon as possible.

Dr. Larsen's habit was to see as many patients as he could on the East Unit between about 7:30 and 9:00 A.M. If he missed you, he'd be back about lunchtime. One thing I admired about him was that he saw us every day, even if he had to go looking for us in the cafeteria at dinner. Not all the doctors saw their patients every day.

Every so often I missed Dr. Larsen in the morning; then I'd see him at 12:45 or thereabouts. But once, his whole day had fallen apart, and he didn't see any of his patients on the East Unit until 4:30. I didn't realize how much I depended on his visits until that day.

But today, I was afraid I'd miss seeing him until lunchtime, and I wanted to be long gone by then.

I was struggling to get my jeans on in a hurry when I heard him talking to a therapist in the hall. In panic, I grabbed my robe and dashed out in the hall, hair tousled, no make-up on, wearing a green robe with blue jeans and socks underneath.

As I bounded out my door, they both looked at me in surprise.

"Don't go anywhere!" I gasped urgently.

Dr. Larsen grinned at me. "Well, look at you! What's up?"

"I want to go home!" I panted, and then laughed, realizing for the first time what a sight I must be.

Dr. Larsen told me to go ahead and go into the doctors' room while he looked in on a patient he had admitted the night before. It seemed like I was going to see the sunset from that room before he got back, but when I looked at my watch, it said 8:10.

He hadn't seated himself before I started in on how well I had done at home, and that I wanted to be discharged. He eagerly agreed, writing out prescriptions and telling me to call him later in the week. He told me Kana was my therapist that morning, and he would take care of the details of my discharge.

I came jumping and dancing out of the doctors' room like Rocky, yelling, "I've been sprung! I've been sprung!" I was elated and oh, so excited.

A large group had gathered, therapists taking vital signs, the med nurse giving out morning medications, and patients waiting for Dr. Larsen.

A loud cheer broke out as everyone congratulated me. As I moved through them and past them, I saw smiling faces everywhere — Kana, Margo, Melissa, and Roger, the therapists; Harriet, the med nurse; the patients — Janet, Jo Anne, Marvin, Kathy, Marcie ... Neil. Neil was standing apart from the others — face down and sober, shoulders hunched, hands half-inside his front pockets. As I ran past them, I thought to myself: I've got to talk to Neil before I leave.

I hurriedly finished dressing and found Neil still by the nurses' station, waiting to see the doctor. I smiled a brilliant, happy, victorious smile at him, but he didn't return it. That's when I thought of the word "haunted" as a description for the expression in his eyes. Only now, they looked more haunted than I'd ever seen them. I stopped smiling as I came up to him.

"I'd like to talk to you before I go," I said.

"That would be nice," he said immediately.

"When would you be available?" I asked him. "I'm going to eat breakfast now. Shall we meet in the cafeteria?"

"Yeah," he answered, softly. "I've gotta see the doctor first."

In the cafeteria, I couldn't sit still. After downing a glass of milk, I was back on the East Unit. Neil was still waiting. Before I spoke, Kana grabbed my arm. He was from India, and I really enjoyed the days I had him as a therapist.

"I have a meeting now, but when I get out ... mmm ... about 9:30, I want to discharge you. We'll have to hurry, because I've got group therapy at 10:15."

I looked at my watch. It said 8:45. Neil had overheard our conversation.

"I'm still waiting," he said, desperately.

"Okay. I haven't packed yet. I'll go pack; that shouldn't take me long," I told him. I felt like my world was going in fast motion.

"Will you find me in the cafeteria if I'm not here when you're done?" he asked, his voice pleading.

"Yeah ... if I don't come to the cafeteria, I'll be here on the unit somewhere, probably in my room."

I started to run down the hall, but something made me turn back. Neil was looking after me, one hand in a tight fist, the other pushing through his hair, nervously.

I went back and touched his arm. "Neil, I won't leave until I talk to you. We'll get together."

He nodded, looking down, chewing on his lower lip. While I ran back to my room to pack, I remember thinking that I had little idea of what I was going to say to him.

22

When I heard him asking for me outside my room, I rushed out and he suggested we take a walk.

Once outside, I started out by telling him he was one of those people in my life that I'd always wonder what happened to.

"I'll wonder if you decided to go to school after all, and if your legal problems got worked out, and most of all, if you're happy."

I took a breath. "I want you to know that you've helped me here in the hospital far more than you'll ever know ..."

A gasp interrupted me, and he blurted, "I didn't think I'd helped you at all. You always seemed to have it all together." His face had a look of shock.

It was my turn to gasp. "Oh no, Neil! I've felt down and beaten much of the time here, and you've shown me over and over that it's possible to get right back up and try again. I needed that."

Neil had set a pretty brisk pace, and I was getting out of breath. I knew there was more I wanted to say, and my tongue seemed to go as fast as my feet.

So when I said, "Neil, I'm afraid for you," it sounded more desperate than I intended it to.

Throughout our conversation, Neil walked with his hands half-way in the front pockets of his jeans and with his head down. Now, he looked at me in alarm, but then looked quickly back at the sidewalk.

"I understand that sometimes you have to go with your instincts, even when everyone says you're wrong or foolish," I ventured carefully, knowing I was treading on sensitive ground.

"And if your plans to sue the government and the Portland police are motivated by a desire to make the world a better place, so that no one else will have to go through what you've gone through," I continued, "then great! Go for it."

I gulped in apprehension. "But if it's motivated by hate, I'm afraid it'll destroy you, and it won't do a thing to the government or police ..."

I trailed off as he stopped, red-faced, with a stricken look on his face. I thought for an instant that he would blast me as he had so many others who tried to discourage him in his plans for revenge.

"It's hate, isn't it?!" he said in a shrill, anguished voice. Before I had time to respond, he strode on without me, his hands holding his head, shouting, "Oh God! It's hate! Oh God! ... Oh God!"

Greatly surprised, I stood still, uncertain. As he continued on down the sidewalk without me, I knew I couldn't leave him like that. I had to run to catch up with him.

"That hate is tearing you up inside, Neil," I panted, "and it's a painful thing to see."

He put his hands back in his pockets in his characteristic way, breathing heavily, eyes cast down. "I guess I want my cake and eat it, too," he said, reflectively. "I've screwed up everywhere. If I hadn't gone to Fort Steilacoom, I wouldn't have had my nervous breakdown. If I hadn't gone to the V.A. Hospital in Portland, I wouldn't have been taking the meds that messed me up. Maybe if I'd talked to people different. Maybe if I'd fought against going to Nam ... there doesn't seem to be a place where I belong, where what I do is right. Maybe if I hadn't left Oakland and gone to Tacoma ... I always have all these crazy plans ..."

I listened with growing dismay and hurt. All this time I was vaguely aware of a gardener sweeping dead leaves into a basket and two neighbors were out in a yard chatting — that was going on in the periphery of my mind.   What was really taking up my attention was the pain that was growing bigger and bigger, starting in my chest and ending in a growing ache in my eyes, and spilling out onto my cheeks.

I couldn't stand the hurt of this gentle, good person, berating himself for something he couldn't help. Suddenly, I ran around Neil, facing him, and I grabbed his arms, stopping him in his tracks.

"It's not your fault!" I cried, more tears cascading down my face. I was really surprised at myself, but my unusual behavior didn't seem to make a dent in Neil at all. He stood stock still, hands still in his pockets, haunted eyes still on the sidewalk.

"Neil," I said, seeking eye contact, "IT'S NOT YOUR FAULT!" I repeated the words slowly and deliberately, hoping that somehow my words would become tangible and lodge in his mind, making their home there.

Slowly, his eyes came up and met mine. His eyebrows came down, and his eyes registered confusion. Hoping to gain control over my crying, I dropped my hands, took my place beside him, and we started walking again.

"You've had a really rough time for a long, long while," I started out shakily, "and you're just responding to that. Nobody could go through what you've gone through and just shrug his shoulders over it. Any <u>normal</u> person would act much as you have. I suspect your plans are a sort of grief process, to make some sense out of all those years you feel were so empty and wasted. I also suspect you're more normal than you think."

By this time I was wiping my tears and speaking more forcefully.

"And I'm going to make a commitment to you, Neil. I'll always be for you. I'll always be on your side. I may not agree with what you say or do, but that's separate and apart from <u>NEIL</u>. I'll always be for <u>NEIL</u>. So," making an attempt at some levity, "if you get completely paranoid, it'll be your own fault, because there will always be at least one person looking out for your welfare besides yourself."

I smiled at him, but if I was hoping for a shared joke, I was to be disappointed. The face that looked back at me was a study.

"You mean," he said slowly, "even if I did something you didn't like, you wouldn't turn on me? I mean, what if I did something crazy like hold hostages or hit somebody or something or..."

"Oh, Neil," I interrupted," that would be so uncharacteristic of you. I'd think you'd be awfully desperate to be capable of such violence. I wouldn't like it or approve of it, most likely, but I'd <u>still</u> care about you and be interested in your welfare. I'd still be on your side, even if I didn't agree with what you were doing, because we all make mistakes. I make mistakes, and I hope people will still want the best for me, even when they disagree with me."

We walked in silence for a bit. I don't know what Neil was thinking, but I felt like I was taking part in a dramatic scene in a movie. It didn't seem real. I was wondering where these words that were coming out of my mouth were coming from. Instead of originating in my brain and going through normal channels to my tongue, they seemed to originate from my tongue while my brain looked on in amazement.

Neil had picked up the walking pace again. "I should have had you around the last 13 years. I've had doctors tell me I had a bad attitude, and counselors who said to just go out and get a job, and friends who said 'Snap out of it; an evening with you is like watching 60 Minutes.' I tried to snap out of being depressed; I tried everything, and it just got worse, and I felt so alone, like no one cared, no one wanted me. Maybe some of them did care, but I was so bombed out in my depression, I thought their rejection of my ideas was rejection of me. So, I turned away from everybody who disagreed with me, and I thought all I had was ME. I guess I screwed up with that, too."

At this point I remember the bushes on my left side that lined the parking lot's east side. We must have been around the block at least once, maybe twice. I remember, too, that I was out of breath again, and I thought maybe I could just wind this up and go inside and finish my discharge.

But almost in spite of myself, I said, "Neil, I want to tell you something. Religion is a very personal subject with me, and I find it a hard thing to share. I hate seeing these fat, overbearing preachers with white shoes that you see on television yelling, 'Repent!' I don't associate that with a very real relationship with God, and it bothers me that that seems to be a stereotype of religion.

"But I want to share with you that I was one of those lucky people that grew up in a religious family. In a very natural and gradual way, I developed a close relationship with God that has gotten me through some very rough times. There wasn't any climactic moment when I knew God existed; He just always has for me.

"But when my depression hit, my faith, or my idea of my faith, strong as I thought it was, flew right out the window. That was a real source of anxiety for me. I couldn't pray, and I <u>felt</u> in a deep sense that not even God was there for me. I've got friends and family who showed their concern in 100 ways, but I felt alone and unloved.

"Remember when you told me one symptom of depression is withdrawing from people and wanting to be alone all the time?" At his nod, I continued. "Well, I'm thinking that maybe in depression, something goes haywire in our brain that makes us <u>feel</u> alone and unloved and abandoned, when in reality, we're not. It's the depression telling us that falsehood, not our natural self or other people ... or God. Neil, I don't think you screwed it up with your friends. You were mishandled, and your depression was preventing you from coping."

I paused to catch my breath. We walked in silence for a bit, then Neil said, "I hope when I get to Astoria, I can find some good friends. I hope I find the right church with people my age to relate to; I've been around the wrong kind of people too long."

I smiled at him, but his eyes never left the sidewalk. The worry lines were all over his forehead.

"I think if you read your Bible, you'll be led the right way, Neil. It says that it's God's desire that everyone come to Him. When I was really depressed and desperately searching through my Bible for some answers, I happened on Psalm 139, and that's something I've clung to all through my time here at Riverside. Maybe it'll help you, too. People have a way of disappointing us, but God is always there, even when we're depressed and don't feel His presence at all.

"In fact," I was gasping for breath now, talking fast, "all the Psalms are good to read. Most of them were written by ..." I paused to take a breath and Neil finished for me, "David."

"Right!" I said. "And if anyone had a right to feel paranoid, it was David."

"Yeah," Neil said, eyes still down, nostrils flared, head nodding.

We were coming close to the entrance of the hospital again, maybe for the fourth time. I felt an urgency to leave Neil on a positive note, with hope and optimism. Every moment, every word counted now, and I wanted to pour some confidence into him.

In mock severity, I said, "Neil, I want you to erase those worry tapes in your mind!"

He gave me a half-smile. "Okay."

"I want you to replace them with tapes that tell you that you're a worthwhile person <u>right</u> <u>now</u> — not when you're out of the hospital, not in two years, or five, or ten, but right now, you're a person of great worth. You've become very dear to me, Neil, and I care for you very much."

We were walking up the wheelchair ramp to the entrance to the hospital. We were both breathing like we'd run a marathon.

"You know," he said, rounding the last corner of the ramp, "you've always represented love to me. No one has loved me just because I'm me. I couldn't ever figure you out."

His last statement really threw me. As we were going in the door, I thought to myself: What's to figure out?

We were being let into the East Unit when Neil asked me for my address. "Maybe we could write or something ... I mean ... you said you'd wonder what happened to me ... and ..."

He was starting to stammer, so I said, "Sure! Have you got some paper?"

By this time, we were in the doorway of his room, so I followed him in and sat on his bed. While he looked for a piece of paper, I said, "Hey, send me a postcard from Astoria, okay?"

"Yeah, okay, I will ... uh ... here," he said, handing me a sheet of notebook paper and a pencil.

There was silence as I quickly wrote my name and address. I included Psalm 139, so, hopefully, he'd remember to read it. Then I heard Kana calling me in the hall.

"Hey, listen, I've got to go," I said, jumping up off the bed. "Write me if you feel paranoid, okay? And I'll write right back and tell you you're a good person!"

Neil made a noise halfway between a snort and a chuckle. "Okay."

"And I'm really interested to know how your hearing with the judge goes." I handed him the paper and pencil.

Neil sighed and looked away. After a pause, he said in a strained voice, "I'm ... terrified of seeing that judge."

I couldn't see his face, but his free hand balled into a fist.

"Hey, look," I said, and he looked at me sideways, just with his eyes, turning his head only a fraction. "Tell Dr. Larsen about it, okay? Remember? He's the best. That's what he's here for; he'll make it okay for you, I'm certain of it."

Neil looked down again and just nodded. Then he looked up, eyes boring into mine. We stood there, looking at each other for a bit, and then I said, "Well, do I have to wait two years for a hug?"

"Uh, no," Neil stammered, putting down the paper and pencil on his bed. I wrapped my arms around his chest, because that's as far up as my arms could reach, and he bent over, slowly and carefully, and laid his head on my shoulder, his arms across my shoulder blades. I held him close when I realized he was crying.

Oh God, I prayed, what is going to happen to this very special person? Please take care of him!

Kana called again, so I pulled away. As I started out the door, Neil grabbed my right wrist, unusual for him, one of the few times he touched me.

"Hey ... uh ... it was really nice of you to say all those good things to me. Thanks for ..." he shrugged his shoulders, "... being so nice ..."

"Oh, Neil," I said in exasperation, "I didn't say it to be nice; I said it because it's true, and it needed to be said." I patted him on the upper arm with my free hand. "You're easy to love."

Kana's next call left no doubt that his impatience was getting the better of him. I had to go.

"Bye, Neil," I said, breaking away. "Have a good life!"

I ran into the hall with joy and excitement in my heart at the prospect of going home. But I'll always remember Neil's face as I left. The haunted look in his eyes was replaced with abject pain, and there was a tear running down one cheek. He stood in the doorway, hands forever halfway in his pockets, shoulders slumped, looking (for Neil) very small and vulnerable. It's a scene that will be forever etched in my mind.

23

The details of my actual discharge are blurred and confused in my memory. Everything and everyone seemed to be going in fast motion.

Logan was magically there while Kana asked questions and had me sign papers. Kathy was in and out of my consciousness, asking first if Neil and I had had our "little talk," then wanting my address. To stave her off, I told her I'd given it to Neil. We were almost off the unit when she was back, saying she couldn't find him. I told her, as Kana maneuvered me out the door, that I'd left him in his room.

There were well-wishes from patients and staff, I remember. And there were the rounds to the pharmacy, arts and crafts room, and business office. Then finally, Kana was shaking my hand at the entrance, wishing me all the best.

The sun was shining on our way home. I watched the scenery in silence as we drove home, as if for the first time. I was thinking that this must be how a caterpillar feels when it comes out of the cocoon.

Home ... home ... I was home. Logan went back to work, and Leighton would continue staying with his grandparents that day as he had every day I'd been in the hospital.

I unpacked. I wandered around touching things. I noticed that there were so many things to be done, and I knew I'd be the one to do them. I gloried in my freedom, and I took a Xanax all by myself to celebrate.

Wow, I thought to myself as I made a sandwich, I can still make my own lunch. I watched some television and fell asleep. When I woke up, I stretched and thought happily: I'm home, I'm home. It wasn't a dream.

That evening I greeted Leighton and Logan, happy that I'd be there to stay, and Logan bought us hamburgers to celebrate. As I tidied up the kitchen, I thought to myself: Everything is okay now. I'm home.

It all came crashing down on me when I turned on the television to see what was on. When I saw the football game, suddenly I saw Neil's face as I had left him that morning, and I burst into tears.

I looked all around me, and everything was alien and overwhelming. I ran into our spare bedroom and cried most of the rest of the evening.

Oh, Neil, I thought, are you watching that football game without me? Oh God, please watch over him. Keep him safe.

The next morning I was able to get Leighton up, dressed, and fed before Logan's dad came to take him away for the morning. Victory! I tidied the house and exercised. Maybe things wouldn't be so bad after all.

That afternoon, after I laid Leighton down for a nap, I tried to read, but all I could see was Neil's face. He'd be in Arts and Crafts now, I was thinking. And I started crying again. I felt like a mother who had sent her child off to kindergarten for the first time; only I probably wouldn't know how he was faring for a long time, if ever.

Oh God, I'd pray, I pass the baton to You. Please watch over him. But I kept snatching him back.

The first week went on much like this while I tried to find my way in my own life. Sometimes I'd pause in a household task and wail, "God. Neil ... I'm so worried about Neil!"

It was during one such call to God that I saw an image. It was Neil, walking through an obstacle course just like the one he walked through in the hospital, only I wasn't the one directing him — God was. It was as if He had His arms around Neil — no — more than that. Neil had an aura around him that was leading him. He still looked worried and sweaty, but, nevertheless, he was being led safely around trouble.

The meaning was obvious to me. God was telling me He was leading Neil through life, and I was not to worry. I still worried, but I wasn't in anguish over him anymore. I knew it was now up to me to trust.

So, when I was tempted to wring my hands, I thought of Neil being led by God. And I knew that same guidance was surrounding me, too. Now, I was just lonely for his friendship. I hoped he'd be able to get out of the hospital and write to me soon.

Several days later, I was lying on my bed, looking out the window into the blue sky. The sun was shining, and I was feeling warm and content. I was thinking about which books I wanted to store and which to keep in a bookcase when suddenly I saw Neil's face floating in the sky, slowly, slowly, floating higher and higher. It was just his face, and it held the

joyful expression I'd seen after he'd made it success-
fully to his chair after the obstacle course exercise.

I smiled peacefully at it, and afterward wondered what it meant. "I hope this doesn't mean that
he's going to die," I said nervously to my sister, Sharon, long-distance on the phone.

"Maybe this means he'll be going to Heaven
when he does die," she suggested. Sharon had been
avidly keeping up with my experiences with Neil. In
fact, she had shared Neil with several friends of hers
and all were praying for him.

I laughed when I learned of this. If Neil only
knew the attention his life was getting, he'd be in
shock for weeks. And this led to the questions: Why
am I so obsessed with Neil? Why is the story of Neil so
powerful?

I had no answers, and as the days went on, I
found myself needing to know how Neil was doing--not
because I wasn't trusting God to care for him, but because I needed to know what and how he was doing. I
just needed the knowledge, like one needs to know the
ending of a book.

On the third week after my discharge, I found
out.

24

It was Tuesday, the day Neil was supposed to appear before the judge. All morning I was nervous, and I attributed the anxiety to the fact that I was in the difficult part of my menstrual cycle. I also knew that this was the day that a part of Neil's future would be decided.

The mail came that afternoon about 1:30. When I saw Kathy's name on the upper left-hand corner of the envelope, I had mixed feelings. My stomach churned, and with a feeling of dread, I tore it open.

I hastily read it, hungry for news of Neil. It was written in a large, immature scrawl, not making a whole lot of sense. It was two pages of rambling, misspelled, and disorganized thoughts.

She said she and Marvin and Neil all wanted to be good friends with me; that Mikey's birthday party had been a success, and that her family thought Neil was a "terrific guy." She said she and Neil laughed a lot about her two-year rule and that she had found Neil to be very "huggable and kissable." They were glad to be out of the hospital because now they could see each other so much more. She also said Neil was going to spend all the major holidays with her family.

She went on and on about what she was doing to "stay well," but there was no more about Neil — no

word on his legal problems or how he was feeling —
just that he was going to leave for Astoria on Friday.

The next morning a letter to Kathy went out
from me. I congratulated her on her discharge and included a message to Neil, reminding him that he
meant a lot to me and that he had promised me a postcard from Astoria.

This was a round-about way of communicating,
I felt, but better than none at all.

I was jumping on my mini-jogger the next morning —Thursday — when Kathy called. I knew who she
was before she told me — her voice had the familiar
machine-gun-fire quality to it. I also knew, with a
tightening of my stomach, that something was wrong,
because there was a distraught, panicked air in her
voice that I hadn't heard before.

"Oh, Judy, this is Kathy. I'm so upset and concerned about Neil. He called me Monday night and
said he hadn't slept in two days and couldn't sleep,
and he'd taken forty of his pills to try to get to sleep,
but couldn't. And he said he was so tired of being
messed up, and he didn't want to live anymore. And
he said he wouldn't make a good husband, worse than
Gary to me! We were going to get engaged in six
months and married in a year. I kept telling him to
<u>talk</u>, <u>talk</u>, <u>talk</u> to me, but he said he didn't want to see
me for a few days, to pull himself together. He didn't
want me to see him like he was. But when I looked for
him at Meier & Frank's, he didn't come, and I've called
the police and they say there aren't any unidentified
dead bodies. I went looking for him with my step-dad
at the address he gave me where he lives with Vaughn,
but we couldn't find it, and the police won't."

"Kathy, Kathy," I was trying to break in. "You say Neil took forty of his pills?" I found myself taking notes. This was confusing, and I wanted to get my facts straight.

"No, I think he said four or five, oh, I don't know, maybe more, but I'm afraid he's dead on the street somewhere! The police won't go to the address to find him, because they say he hasn't done anything."

Which is just as well, I thought to myself, considering how Neil feels about the police.

"Maybe he just needs some time alone," I suggested. Heaven knows, even Neil must have a limit on how long he could put up with Kathy's behavior. "Wouldn't his roommate have called you if something was wrong?"

"Oh no!" she said, shrilly. "He hates me! He's queer and jealous of me. Neil said he never bothered him, though. And when he was real sick before, Neil said Vaughn took real good care of him."

I started getting a headache and was rubbing my forehead. Also, her panic was starting to transmit itself through the phone. I was still thinking about the pills.

"Listen, Kathy," I said. "When Neil called you, did you call Dr. Larsen?"

"No!" she screamed. "We don't want him to know about us! He says I have too many men!"

I put the phone to my throbbing forehead. I think if we had been talking face to face, I would have shaken her until all her teeth fell out. To put her own feelings above Neil's welfare was unthinkable to me.

When I put the phone back to my ear, she was saying something about limiting Hank's visits to twice a week. "Kathy," I broke in, "I'm going to call Dr. Larsen."

"NO!" she screamed, sounding hysterical. "You can't, you can't ..."

"Kathy, listen to me! Maybe he knows something. And if he doesn't, he ought to. He's Neil's doctor!"

She went on pleading with me, saying the same things over and over, so I looked at my notes.

"Kathy," I interrupted, "why were you waiting for Neil at Meier and Frank?"

She told me that the previous weekend, they had decided to meet in front of the department store after Neil had had the hearing with the judge, but though she waited two hours, he never showed up.

"Could he have gone on to Astoria?" I asked.

"No, I called Marvin, and he hadn't seen him. Oh, Judy, couldn't you go try to find the address?"

So, I thought, Marvin is out of the hospital, too.

"NO," I answered. "I don't have any transportation during the day. I'm calling Dr. Larsen."

I finally got her to end the conversation by telling her I wouldn't tell him who had called me unless he specifically asked.

I put the call in and spent the hours it took for Dr. Larsen to return my call by alternately praying urgently and remembering my image of Neil being surrounded by God's aura of guidance.

Kathy called several times in the interim, causing me to be both disappointed and angry. I'd jump for the phone, expecting the doctor. Instead, I'd hear the same fast, distraught voice. My day was turning into a nightmare of telephone rings.

Our conversations took on a pattern. She'd ask me if I'd heard anything, and I'd assure her that I hadn't and would let her know as soon as I had.

"When did you and Neil get out of the hospital?" I asked her during one of her calls.

"On the 17th — the day of Mikey's birthday party. We were so glad to get out. Everybody was talking about us because we were so close. Marvin teased us a lot. But we're really in love."

The 17th, I mused. That was the Saturday after the Monday I was discharged.

"Judy, what did you and Neil talk about the day you got out of the hospital?" she asked, abruptly.

"Why don't you ask Neil?" I countered, surprised.

"He said he didn't want to talk about it."

"Well, then, I guess that's between you and Neil. Have you tried calling Vaughn?" I asked, changing the subject.

"He doesn't have a phone," she whined. "Neil had to call from a phone booth eight blocks away. Oh, Judy, I'm so worried!"

So am I, I thought silently. So am I.

When Dr. Larsen returned the call about 2:30, I was pleasantly surprised, thinking it was Kathy's dialing finger getting itchy again. I told him that I had found myself in the middle of an awkward situation, and since he knew everybody involved, I was going to throw it in his lap.

He laughed. "Thanks a lot!"

I told him of Kathy's calls; how I thought she was out of touch with reality most of the time; my concern for Neil; and that I felt a responsibility to let him know about Neil.

"Judy," Dr. Larsen said, crisply, "you did the right thing by calling me. You must understand that I can't discuss with you either of these cases, but I will tell you that your estimation of Kathy is correct and that I am aware of Neil's condition. I also don't want you to have anything to do with these people; it can cause you nothing but grief. If you hear from Kathy again, refer her to me. Don't waste your time talking to her — it won't do either of you any good."

"Okay," I said, relieved. "I understand all this patient confidentiality stuff, but can you at least tell me Neil is okay?"

"No," he said, quickly. "Neil is not okay. So how are you doing?"

Hmmmm, I thought to myself, Neil must be on the West Unit. Or is he? How bad off _is_ he?

"I have agonized all day about Neil's welfare," I began, impatient with Dr. Larsen's manner. I wasn't thinking, then, that he knew nothing of my emotional investment in Neil, "You can't leave me like this! Is he at least under some kind of care?"

I heard a sigh. "Judy," Dr. Larsen said, then paused. "Neil died of an accidental overdose of the drugs he had, earlier this week."

It was as if a giant hand had squeezed my torso, forcing all the air out. I managed a small, whimpering, "Oh..."

"Now, I don't want you to fret about this ..." he began.

"Fret? Don't fret?" I got my air back in a hurry. "Ask me to jump over the moon and that would be more likely! I cared for Neil; this has really upset me! You don't want me to fret?"

"Judy, listen to me," Dr. Larsen broke in, authoritatively. "I told you this because I know you can handle it. I was afraid you'd read it in the newspaper, and maybe it would be easier if you heard it from me."

I remember sitting on the bed with the phone to my ear, nervously tracing the pattern of the bedspread with my finger. My eyes weren't focusing on anything, and my mind was struggling to comprehend the words coming through the receiver.

"There wasn't anything anybody could do; it's just one of those tragic things that happen," Dr. Larsen was saying. "I want you to remember that, and we'll talk about it next week when you come in to see me."

"Okay," I said softly. Without waiting for him to say goodbye, I hung up.

I sat there a long time. What do I do now? I asked myself. What do I do now? Shouldn't I be crying or something?

I got up and walked around the house. I picked up a pen to write in my journal, but my hands were shaking so much I couldn't write. The pen just dropped out of my hand.

I walked out the back door and walked around the backyard. I kept thinking that I didn't know how to feel. I'd try this feeling and that feeling, but nothing surfaced — no sorrow, no anger, no nothing. It was like I was trying all the keys on an unplugged typewriter — nothing was happening. All my electricity was gone. My body was in the middle of one long gasp. I had the feeling that if I pricked myself with a pin, I wouldn't feel it.

After a while, I remembered I was supposed to call Kathy, and I went indoors. I picked up the phone but found I couldn't dial. I took a Xanax, walked around some more and formed my words.

"Kathy," I said as calmly and as naturally as I could manage, "Dr. Larsen called. He said he was aware of Neil's condition, and he told me not to fret. He said if you wanted to know more, you can call him."

"Oh! Is Neil okay? Is he back in the hospital?" she asked, frantically.

"I can't tell you any more," I said, mechanically, feeling like a robot. "Just call Dr. Larsen."

"Did you tell him about us?"

"Kathy, I had to. I was concerned for Neil's welfare. It doesn't make a whole lot of sense to me, anyway," I said, getting angry. "You're seeing a doctor to get better, and you're not being up front with him! Just call Dr. Larsen, okay? I can't tell you any more than what I've already said." I wanted the conversation to end. I was desperate to hang up. Reluctantly, she gave up.

I paced around the house some more. I needed to keep moving. I had the feeling that if I stopped moving, I'd suffocate.

Leighton woke up from his nap early. He was crying and calling my name. Grateful for something constructive to do, I hurried to his room.

This was unusual. Usually, Leighton woke up happy and cheerful. Now, his face was flushed, he was crying, and he lifted up his arms to me.

Gently, I picked him up and cradled him close to me. Carrying him to the rocking chair, I could tell he had a bit of a fever. He snuggled down against me, and we rocked.

As I caressed the hair from his face, I wondered in my numbness if Neil's mother had done that to a little Neil, loving him, worrying over his childhood illnesses, wondering how he'd turn out. I wondered how she felt about his adult problems and whether somewhere there was a mother crying in grief over her son. I wished I could tell her how good and kind and considerate and eager to be better he was. I wished I could share her grief. I thought about all that as I rocked Leighton, grateful that he was still young enough to rock and comfort and hold in my arms.

Since Logan had to work evenings all that week, we had arranged for Leighton to stay at his grandparents' house those evenings to give me a break. A couple of hours in the rocking chair and some Tylenol seemed to have done the trick, because Leighton was happy to go when Logan's mother came by for him.

Alone again, I stood at the kitchen sink and stared out the window for a long time. I could see into the backyard of our neighbor. He'd done a good job improving the wooden fence on the other side of his yard, I noted. His half-grown German shepherd sat on their picnic table, his ears twitching. As I saw the stars start to twinkle on, one by one, I asked myself over and over: What do I do now?

After a while, I remembered the story of David in the Bible. After his infant son had died, he got up and got dressed and ordered some food to eat. And his servants were amazed at his behavior because while the child was alive, he fasted and wept. But now that the child was dead, he got up and ate.

But David explained it this way:

"While the child was still alive, I fasted and wept. I thought, 'who knows? The Lord may be gracious to me and let the child live.' But now that he is dead, why should I fast? Can I bring him back again? I will go to him, but he will not return to me." (2 Sam. 12:22-23)

So, I made myself a roast beef sandwich and poured a glass of milk. As I ate, I thought: Goodbye, Neil. I've got to pick up my life as best I can and go on. Goodbye, Neil ... goodbye ... I felt a great wistfulness.

It seemed important to do the ordinary things. I washed the dishes and tidied the kitchen. I turned on the television, but I don't remember what was on.

When the phone rang, I jumped, realizing I'd been staring into space for a long time. It was Kathy again. Apparently, Dr. Larsen hadn't returned her call. I tried to reassure her that he'd call soon, or maybe tomorrow.

"What do you think, Judy? Is Neil okay? Is Dr. Larsen taking care of him?" Her voice whined in my ear.

"It doesn't matter what I think," I began.

"But don't you think if Dr. Larsen knows about Neil that he's taking care of him?" Kathy asked, urgently.

I could well understand her urgency. I'd feel it, too, if the situation were reversed. As kindly as I could, I tried to reassure her without giving her false hopes.

"Kathy, what I think doesn't matter; it doesn't have anything to do with reality. I'm sure Dr. Larsen will call you soon and he'll tell you all about Neil's condition."

"Judy, what were you to Neil?" she asked, throwing me off guard.

I hesitated. "We were good friends," I said, haltingly.

"He said you were very special to him."

"Well ... he was very special to me, too," I said, bewildered, wondering if she was noticing we were talking about him in the past tense.

"Was he your boyfriend?" she asked, getting more agitated.

"No!" I denied, tears of frustration stinging my eyes. "I'm very happily married! Neil was a very special person to me, but only as a friend. Only as a very special friend!"

She started to whine again. "Neil said that the only girl he ever wanted to marry was already married. Was that you?"

"NO!" I wailed. "Neil and I were only very good friends! We talked about our relationship, and I'm certain he only thought of me as a friend."

Oh, what's the use, I thought, as tears started running down my cheeks. It's a moot point, now. Talking to Kathy is like trying to pour water into a bucket full of holes.

"We were going to get married, Judy! Can't you understand how I need to know about him? I'm so worried!" Kathy shouted.

I wondered if she was talking about being worried about my relationship with him or being worried about his welfare. I chose to comment on the latter.

"Listen, I've been in anguish over Neil since you first called," I said. "I understand how you could be upset over him after not hearing from him. But there's nothing we can do now. We'd better get off the phone now. Dr. Larsen is probably trying to call you."

She hastily agreed.

I started pacing. The phone rang twice more, but they were only good friends calling about how I was doing. I jumped every time the phone rang, wondering if I should unplug it, only to decide against it in case Logan needed to call or if his folks needed to contact me about Leighton.

"Fine," I'd say to those people who called. "I'm getting better."

What else could I say? I couldn't feel anything but tension. I felt like an undefined word.

As I paced, I started thinking that I hadn't realized how much a habit agonizing and praying over Neil had become. I'd begin to worry and then remember with a start that he was dead — it's all over — and I'd feel like someone punched me in the stomach.

In a way, I thought, it's a relief. I thought it was all over. But in many ways, it was just beginning.

25

By the time Logan and Leighton got home, I was a bundle of nerves. I had begun to look at the phone as an enemy and was jumping at every sound.

After Leighton was put to bed, I told Logan about Neil, and the tears finally came. I could feel them glancing off my cheeks and falling on my lap.

"Oh, Jude, I'm so sorry," Logan said softly, as I wiped my nose.

"Why does everyone I care about die suddenly?" I sobbed. "It's so rude when people die like that!"

A little later I asked, "Log, where's Neil now? Don't you think if I loved him so much, God does, too?"

I looked up from his chest, and Logan was looking straight ahead, his arms around me. "I don't know, Jude. I wish I could say something that would make you feel better. I just don't know."

After a time, I couldn't sit still anymore, and Logan went off to bed. He had had a long day.

I paced back and forth in the living room, tears soaking my face. Why, Neil? Why did you call Kathy? Why didn't you call Dr. Larsen? Why didn't you call me? You didn't even say goodbye! I told you that you were a survivor, and look what you did! How could I have been so wrong? What happened to you? What happened?!

Oh, God, I prayed, I can't stand the thought of Neil being in hell after the hell he's lived here on earth. Oh Lord, he was sick! He was looking for you! He acknowledged you! Was that enough?

I started remembering preachers from my childhood arguing that the only true church was the one they attended, that baptism was the only salvation. Everyone else was hell-bound if they didn't attend church three times a week. I remembered stories about teenagers who said they'd get baptized next Sunday and they were killed in car accidents during the week, and everyone <u>knew</u> they'd gone straight to their doom. These thoughts were like buzzards picking at my emotions, and I felt like screaming. I paced back and forth with my hands over my ears, trying to silence the voices that went on and on.

Then came the inevitable "what ifs." What if I had put my phone number down under my address that I had given to Neil? What if I had emphasized his calling me if it all fell apart for him? But he had a doctor for that, I reasoned. Why, Neil? Why didn't you call Dr. Larsen?

What if I had stayed that extra week like he wanted me to? Would it have made a difference? But I always came back to no for an answer. I <u>had</u> to go home. My first responsibility was to my family; and besides, I couldn't take being in the hospital any longer.

Was it my fault, Lord? Was I put there to "convert" Neil, and I failed somehow? Oh Lord, you knew my condition in the hospital! I was barely intact. Why, Lord? How could this have happened?

Sometime, just before dawn, Dr. Larsen's words were played back in my mind — "an accidental overdose of the drugs he had." I stopped pacing and leaned over on the dining room table. Nothing was said about suicide, but that was what I heard — what I had understood — when Dr. Larsen told me.

I straightened up and wiped one eye with the back of my hand. An accident? You mean, maybe, you accidentally died, Neil?

It didn't bring me much more comfort. How could that happen, Lord? An accident?! After all my prayers? After so many people were praying for him? He accidentally died?! Maybe you didn't mean to die at all, Neil; I'm so sorry I wasn't enough! Oh God, this is so hard to understand!

I started pacing again, and Jesus' words came to me — the same ones He asked his apostles while in Capernaum when many of the disciples left: "Will you leave me also?" I stopped in my tracks, rubbing my aching eyes. After a moment, I laid down on the couch, considering.

I at last had to say, like Peter, "Lord, to whom shall I go? You have the words of eternal life." I added, however, "But this is under protest; You know how I feel. I'm in torment. But I have no alternative. I have nowhere else to go. You have truth, though I don't understand it. I don't understand it at all."

Sleep only came with exhaustion that morning.

26

I sat up with a start when the phone rang. I rubbed my eyes as I looked at the clock — almost 9:00. Somehow, I had made it to bed in the early morning hours. Logan was talking on the phone.

I was confused. Something awful had happened. And why was Logan home?

Oh yeah ... I laid back down on my pillow, my hands feeling cool over my hot, swollen eyes. Neil had died. And Logan had said he'd stay home this morning in case Kathy called. I just couldn't face talking to her.

I dully picked up where I left off several hours earlier. An accident. It had to be an accident. Neil had grown so much in the hospital. And he had had all those plans. He had been so adamant about seeking help if things went wrong again. What a lot to give he had had; he was one of those rare people that showed his good side as second nature. And now it was all over. What a waste!

Logan came in the bedroom to tell me Kathy called to say Dr. Larsen still hadn't called, was sorry to hear I wasn't feeling well, and that she would be praying for me.

Fresh tears came as I buried my head in my pillow. It was I who should be praying for her. What a lot of grief she was in for. Kathy, Kathy, I railed silently, why didn't you call Dr. Larsen when Neil called? How could you put your own feelings above Neil's welfare?

Logan's dad came by to take Leighton on an outing for the morning, and Logan went on to work. I mechanically dressed and ate and tidied up, but pain dominated my thoughts.

This makes no sense at all, Lord. What part do You play in accidents? I've been in prayer over Neil since I got out of the hospital! Why? Why? Why did it happen this way?

It had been suggested that I was put in the hospital to be a light to Neil — to point the way to God for him. I laughed it off, saying it hadn't been worth all the pain I had been through. Now, the scheme of things really made no sense. Before, much of the time when I'd been feeling low, I'd think of Neil as a positive part of my hospitalization. He was my friend. I had needed him as much as he had needed me. Now even that was stripped from me.

Dr. Larsen called to ask how I was doing. I told him I had felt better. He told me to get some rest, that we'd talk next week, and that I'd be fine.

Fine ... I doubted that I'd ever be fine. When I had dealt with sudden death before, all I had had to deal with was my response — my own personal grief. I always knew that my grandmother, my father, my brother-in-law, my friend in college, a co-worker were saved — I always knew they were with God. My grief was largely self-centered in that I felt loss because there was a hole in my life without them.

With Neil, it was reversed. I never really thought I'd see Neil again — maybe hear from him a few times

— but I had accepted that once I knew he was doing okay, we'd be going our own ways.

Now my grief was tied up in Neil's salvation. My torment was relentless. If I had seen him kick dogs or spit on babies or do something inherently cruel, it still would have been hard, but I could have accepted with less pain that there was a possibility that he wasn't with God and that I'd never see him again.

In my anguish, I remembered that I had relinquished long ago all feelings of judging the ultimate destination of people. It says in the Bible that "God will save who He will," and I figured that since He made up the rules, He could save anybody He wants to. It wasn't up to me.

But in Neil's case, I found myself praying over and over: "He had such a rough time here on earth and yet he was so good and kind, Lord. Doesn't that count for anything?" I felt like a lawyer, pleading his case. In Neil's case I had to know where he was now, and therein lay the core of my torment. The fact that he died as the result of an accident added more weight to my anguish.

That afternoon's mail brought my Guideposts magazine. Anxious for something to distract me, I bedded Leighton down for his nap, and then settled myself down to read.

The first article was about someone going through some kind of problem (I had trouble concentrating), but a scripture he used caught my eye. It was Job saying, "Though He slay me, still will I trust Him."

I jumped off the bed and looked out the window. It was one of those rare cloudless days we get in Portland when the sky is a brilliant blue, and I pondered as I scrutinized that blue sky.

That's what it all boils down to, isn't it, Lord? Trust. Oh, I'm not so puffed up that I think the pain I'm feeling has never been felt before. David felt it. Job felt it. Elijah felt it. I'm not the only one throughout all the generations that separate me from them that shook my fist in the face of God and asked, "Why?" I can name a dozen contemporaries that have felt my pain and worse.

God, I've been through the "refiner's fire" and I don't feel any closer to being like You. I'm in unbearable torment over Neil, Lord. I can't stand the thought of him being in hell. Sometimes I've felt like I couldn't breathe another breath, because I don't know what my response is supposed to be.

But now I know — trust. I don't have any idea of what's going on here. I don't have any idea of what's going to happen. I may live in torment like this the rest of my life. You know I'm not happy; I can't hide that from You. But, nevertheless, I'll stand with Job and say that though You kill me, I'll still trust You.

I rubbed the backs of my hands across my wet eyes, still hurting, still in anguish, but not expecting any relief anymore. I felt like the ball was in God's court now. All I had to do was trust Him to throw it back, sometime, if He wanted to, in His own way.

I slowly laid back down on the bed. I was reading several articles later about some lady who was having trouble with the annoying habit of biting her nails, when I saw him.

The magazine dropped unnoticed on my chest. My mouth popped open in surprise. My eyes were open, staring at the bookcase, but I saw him just as clearly as if someone were running a video tape in front of me.

It was Neil. He was lying on a couch or a bed and he was sick and calling out. He was so sick, and his arms were raised, begging for help. And God came. God came and picked him up, much as I had picked up a crying, feverish Leighton the day before. God picked up Neil and cradled him against Him, comforting him. And a voice said, "I just took him to myself."

And suddenly I knew that Neil was quite safe.

EPILOGUE

I laid there on the bed for several minutes, re-running my "vision" (for want of a better word) before I grabbed the nearest available pencil and an old envelope from the trash to write down what I heard, so that I wouldn't forget the exact words.

I <u>knew</u> right away what I had seen was from God. I knew, because in one instant my torment was completely gone. I wasn't in anguish anymore. I had been comforted, and I knew it was God who had comforted me. I knew now that Neil was with God, and I wasn't worried about him anymore. I knew that God loved Neil and God loved me. I laid on my bed for a couple of hours letting it sink in, and then I wrote it all in my journal.

It was then that the doubts came. What I had written on paper sounded so weird. Could it have been my medication? Maybe fatigue was playing tricks on me. Or perhaps I was crazy after all. But like a broken record, I kept coming back to the realization that my pain was gone. I looked for it like a tongue looks for a sore place in the mouth, but it was simply not there. It had vanished, and with that knowledge, I had to come to the conclusion that the Comforter had fulfilled His purpose in me.

I had been raised with the idea that the Holy Spirit was only the Bible — nothing more. All the miracles in the Book of Acts had stopped after the Apostles died. I think I was about 12 years old when I rejected that idea. There was simply too much evidence that pointed otherwise. But, being the type of person I was, I kept my ideas to myself, avoiding conflict.

Many times I felt myself prompted to do or to say something to someone, and then that someone would express to me later that what I had done or said was just what they had needed. I felt then that that was the Holy Spirit working in me, and I still think so.

After Leighton was born, I found myself in great despair because I never had any time to study the scriptures as I was used to, and my prayers became prayers on the run — "Oh Lord, please ease Leighton back to sleep." "God, if he's crying about something that's serious, please make it obvious to me." "Lord, please make tonight the night he sleeps all the way through."

After one particularly hard afternoon, I was walking the floor with Leighton screaming over my shoulder, and I cried out aloud, "Lord, how am I supposed to stay close to You if I can't have a minute to myself to read the Bible?"

And a voice, an ordinary voice, said inside my head, "My grace is sufficient unto you."

It was as if someone had splashed cold water in my face. I remember thinking that I thought that was in the Bible. It was several weeks later before I had a chance to look it up.

It was in II Corinthians, and Paul was talking about his thorn in the flesh. And the comment about his grace being sufficient is followed by the statement that in our weakness God's power is made perfect. The message was clear to me: My staying close to Him did not depend entirely on my daily Bible reading. I was consumed with a task right then (and I felt at the time it was <u>my</u> thorn in the flesh), and His grace would carry me. That was a real comfort to me, and I relaxed and studied when I could.

Up until the vision of Neil with God, that voice in my mind was the only overt communication I had had with the Spirit — other than the image I saw of the aura around Neil in the obstacle course, and his face floating in the sky. No obvious voices or pictures — just little nudges to do the right thing and the peace that I was saved.

Since I was troubled about this new experience, I hesitated to share it, even with Logan. This was all so new to me; I was afraid he'd think I had really cracked. Before all this happened, I believed that some people saw visions from God; I had just concluded that He hadn't chosen that method of communicating with me. I didn't know what Logan's thoughts were; we'd never discussed it. But, it was such a profound experience, and since I kept coming back to the conclusion that it was of God, I found myself asking Logan at the first opportunity if he believed in visions.

Logan is a real Bible scholar, and sometimes I stand in awe at his knowledge and insights, and I'm not alone in feeling that way. Many people have told me how much they've appreciated thoughts he has shared. That evening when I nervously asked him, he characteristically stretched out on the bed, put his arms behind his head, and launched into what he thought in respect to the difference between the mind, the soul, and the Holy Spirit living in us. He ended up by telling me that you have to believe in visions if you read the Book of Acts.

It was then that I told him about God taking Neil[3] and my subsequent loss of pain. Logan's eyes filled with tears. "Jude," he said, "that's such a beautiful picture. I really do think that God uses visions and dreams to communicate with us."

Dreams! I suddenly remembered a dream I had had earlier that week. It was so beautiful that I had written it down in my journal when I woke up — about 5:00 in the morning. I scrambled across the bed to look it up.

Yes — it was early morning on the 25th — the morning before the evening Neil had apparently called Kathy. I had awakened suddenly and the details were so clear, and I felt so good about the dream that I wanted to remember it forever.

I read it to Logan: I was standing on the large porch of a beautiful white turn-of-the-century house, set on a gigantic estate of some sort which had an impeccably landscaped yard. The grass was short and a vivid green, and there were perfect bushes here and there, and flowers in bloom all about. The house was rather large and had gabled windows. It was early morning, and I was dressed in a white long-sleeved dress with lace all over it. It came to just below my knee and was gathered at the waist. The white of the

---

[3] On hearing this, I had to ask the obvious question: What did God look like? And the answer was, He did not look like anything. It was just the knowledge that this was God, doing this.   Logan.

house and of my dress weren't just white — they were blindingly pure, so white they almost sparkled. I looked absolutely stunning, and I knew I did. I walked gracefully to the steps that led to a yard. Off to my right, in the corner of my eye was a gardener, and he was hard at work hoeing something. But, what caught my eye, just as I was going to take the first step down, was Neil. He was on a path that went by the house and kind of curved off in the distance. He was facing the house in his usual stance — hands half-way in the front pockets of his jeans, shoulders hunched, nostrils flared, eyes haunted. He was wearing his black t-shirt and his light-blue and white tennis shoes. I could even see where a breeze was blowing a small portion of his hair on one side. He looked like he was waiting, but he hadn't seen me.

I was overjoyed at seeing him and raised my hand in greeting. But just as I opened my mouth to call to him, I awoke. And I woke up suddenly — no drowsy intermission here. I remember lying in bed and smiling, because it had seemed so real that I really felt I had seen Neil again. I felt so good about it that I decided to write it in my journal right then, before the details got blurred in my mind.

I was perplexed as to the meaning, though. I could see that the house could be Heaven, but what was I doing in Heaven?

"Well, you don't have to be dead to be in the Kingdom of God," Logan said. "The house could be the Kingdom."

"I suppose Neil could have been standing there, close to the Kingdom, waiting to come in," I said, thoughtfully. "I don't know where the gardener fits in, though."

I looked up to see Logan smiling at me. "Oh, I know who the gardener is," he said, pointing at me. "Remember when Mary Magdalene came to the tomb after the resurrection and thought Jesus was a gardener?"
I stared back at Logan, speechless. Goose bumps made me shiver.

***

Kathy called the next morning to say Dr. Larsen had told her about Neil, and she was okay. She was planning to marry the guy and was okay; I, on the other hand, had been an emotional wreck. I tried to accept it all as one of the strange ironies of life and not let it upset me.

When I saw Dr. Larsen the next week, I told him I had come to terms with Neil's death. I didn't tell him about my vision, because I felt he was one of many, many people who wouldn't understand. I did tell him, however, that I had all these sorrowful feelings inside me, but I had nowhere to channel them — no funeral, no grave, not even anybody to write my condolences to. It was as if he'd been whisked away without a trace.

After I explained the relationship Neil and I had had, Dr. Larsen told me that the coroner's report said that Neil had apparently taken several ("maybe three or four") of his anti-depressants. There was also some alcohol in his system, which enhanced the effect the drug had on his nervous system, and he simply stopped breathing sometime late Monday or early Tuesday morning.

There was absolutely no sign of suicide, and the coroner had judged it to be an accidental death. Dr. Larsen concurred, particularly since Neil was to have seen the judge Tuesday, and he had had a history of mixing alcohol with his drugs when under stress. Dr. Larsen found it particularly tragic since it was his opinion that there was an excellent chance that the charges against Neil would be dropped.

Just as I opened my mouth to express my regret that Kathy had not called Dr. Larsen after Neil had made his call to her, Dr. Larsen told me that Kathy had given him a completely different story than the one she gave me. He told me she was very sick and simply did not deal with reality. He advised that I not try to make sense of her; I wasn't trained to communicate with her. It was then that I realized I had a lot of forgiving to do, for I had in a large part held her responsible for Neil's death.

As for Neil's family, they had not been located. I was surprised — nearly two weeks had gone by. Who had Neil used as next of kin on the admittance forms?

Oh Neil, I thought on the way home, it's all so sad. What happened between you and your family that would form such a gulf?

"Log," I said later, "I feel so sorry that Neil is lying in the morgue, unclaimed."

Logan put his arms around me and smiled. "He was claimed, Jude."

True. But even so, his body was still unclaimed, and to me that was one symbol of being abandoned and unloved by his friends and family here on earth. It was as if no one wanted him, even after he died.

Oh Neil, I thought that evening, can you see me from up in Heaven and feel my love and regret?

It was another month before I saw Dr. Larsen again. At the end of our visit, I asked if Neil's family had been located. He said that he presumed so — that was the coroner's job — but he had not heard anything more.

I was perplexed. "Don't you think it's strange that his family wouldn't want to talk to you?"

The doctor shrugged. "I would think so. But stranger things have happened."

I went home feeling empty and disappointed.

***

I was lying on the bed the next afternoon, thinking about an appointment I had with the ophthalmologist later that afternoon. Since being in the hospital, my eyes had ached and watered and were sensitive to light.

I couldn't read, and I felt generally unwell. I was hoping the doctor would find something easy to treat so I could get on with my life with a bit more ease. (He did, indeed, find an infection, gave me some drops, and it was cleared up with no problem.)

I was thinking about all this when the now-familiar voice said in my mind, "Call the coroner."

I sat up in surprise. "Call the coroner?" I said out loud. "I don't know the number; I don't even know how to look it up in the phone book!"

I half expected an answer, but none came; so with a sigh, I got up and opened the phone book.

With surprisingly little trouble, I found "Coroner-Morgue" right under Multnomah, County of. I dialed the number, then hung up. I dialed three numbers, then hung up again.

"Lord," I said out loud again, "I don't know what to say. I'm afraid I'll get the coroner on the phone and not be able to say a word."

Then I remembered the scripture in II Timothy that says, "For God hath not given us the spirit of fear; but of power, and of love, and of a sound mind." I chuckled at the sound mind part, since I felt rather crazy about making this call. But nevertheless, I took a deep breath and dialed again.

When the man answered the phone, I managed to squeak out, my heart thumping, "I'm not sure if this is the right place to call, but I had a friend who died of an accidental overdose of drugs the last week of September, and the last I heard, his family hadn't been located. I was wondering..." I faltered a bit, "if ... uh ... they have been found since."

"What's the subject's name?" he asked.

"Neil McCarthy."

"OH!" he said in a surprised tone of voice. "They were just located this morning!"

"OH!" I said, parroting his surprise. "Uh ... can you tell me if they plan to ship him back east or bury him here or ...?"

"To my knowledge, no plans have been made as yet," he answered, kindly.

"Thank you," I said, hurriedly, and hung up.

I thumped back down on the bed. I don't believe I did this, I thought. What timing! This morning! But six weeks, Neil! Why did it take six weeks?

Now there was someone to mourn besides me. Even though I didn't know his family, I didn't feel so alone anymore. Now even his earthly body would be claimed, and I felt comforted.

***

I don't claim to know the mind of God. Job says, "Who then can understand the thunder of his power?" And Paul, in the book of Romans, broke out into this doxology: "Oh, the depths of the riches of the wisdom and knowledge of God! How unsearchable his judgments, and his paths beyond tracing out! 'Who has known the mind of the Lord? Or who has been his counselor?'" Part of that passage was quoted from Isaiah.

I do, however, feel that God brought Neil and me together for our mutual benefit. I think that I learned once again the lesson that in my weakness, God's power is made perfect. When I was in the hospital, I was broken, groping, and about as beaten as I've ever been in my life. And through all the wreckage of my life, it is my belief that Neil saw God, bright and clear, without any of my pride or self-importance or any kind of personal walls of defense in the way. It is for that reason that
I, myself, cannot take any credit for providing Neil with some of the answers he was seeking.

I think my dream was God telling me that I had done all He had wanted me to do for Neil — simply pointing the way to the kingdom, to God, and that He would do the rest. I wasn't a failure; I wasn't there to "convert" Neil--that was God's job.

I learned from my vision that God is love. He's not the old ogre up there, waiting for us to break a law and then zap us to eternal misery. He longs to comfort us, just as I long to comfort Leighton in his immature weaknesses. He's our Father, and He loves us with more intensity and power than we can understand. I also learned that God not only loved Neil, but He loves me also.

I'll probably never know what happened to Neil between the day of my discharge and the day he died. But, because of my vision, I know I'll see him again; and because I know that, I can pick up my life and go on.

***

I don't know how to end this, because though Neil's journey is ended, I don't know if the aftermath of his life here on earth has come to an end as far as I am concerned. I ran across a scripture the other day that said, "Mourn with them that mourn." I pray often that someday I'll be able to mourn with Neil's family. I don't know how long it had been since any of them had seen him, but it is my strong desire to let them know that he was a sweet, courteous, genuinely good person. It hurts me to think that all they may know about him is that he spent his last days in a psychiatric hospital and died of an overdose of drugs mixed with alcohol. I want them to know there was much more to Neil than that, and I'm certain that if God wills it, we'll

be brought together somehow. I feel much as I did before — the ball is in God's court. There isn't anything
more I can do. If there is, I'm sure God will let me
know.

I wrote this all down for several reasons. Logan
and Sharon urged me to share it, since it's such a
beautiful story of God's love, but I've been reluctant
because of the vision. I don't want it to be misunderstood. I know deep inside myself that it was from God;
I have no doubts about it. But, I don't consider myself
any more spiritual than anyone else who hasn't had a
similar experience. Nor does my faith rest on that vision. If I never hear another voice or see another vision, I will still believe in God and His love for me.

I also wrote Neil's story down for therapy. This
is the only tangible proof I have now that Neil existed
— I have no picture, no letter, no piece of paper with
his handwriting on it — nothing. This is part of my
grieving process. I want to remember Neil and the part
he played in both being my friend in an awful hour of
trial and in indirectly bringing me closer to God.

I've learned many things in this illness, much of
which has nothing to do with Neil — patience, com-
passion, and how much others truly care for me. And
my learning continues. But the most profound lesson
centered on Neil, and I wanted to confine this story to
him. There is so much I don't know of him — his experiences in Vietnam, his relationships with friends
and family, what led up to his death. But I do know
this: He was searching for truth, God took him to Himself, and I'll see him again someday.

POSTSCRIPT

It was the spring following my hospitalizations, late March, my favorite time of year. Winter and cold and starkness in landscape are over, and one doesn't have to bundle up as much to go outdoors. New life is showing itself, and that has always given me new hope for the future. But you'd never know it from the way I was feeling that day. From the moment I woke up, I felt pursued, haunted. Both Leighton and restlessness dogged my steps, and I wandered from room to room, seeking peace and direction until Leighton finally left for preschool.

Relieved at having several hours to myself, I seized the opportunity to make some progress on typing Neil's story. It was ironic, I felt, that I had composed all those pages in just three weeks, and typing it was taking so much longer. I was busier now, able to do more, getting more done; and so Neil's story was put on the back burner — I was typing a page here, a half-page there.

But, I never stopped thinking about Neil. He showed up in my dreams; I started devouring books on Vietnam — no easy task — as of this writing, there aren't that many books on Vietnam around; stories on the news about the Vietnam Memorial in Washington

D.C. made me cry. I felt that Neil was a casualty of
Vietnam, just as surely as if he had been killed in ac-
tion.

As I became more knowledgeable about Vietnam veterans, I came to a certain peace and understanding of Neil's death. Unlike stories of World War
II, the Civil War, and other catastrophic events of history of which I had read, tales of Vietnam were remark-
ably similar. You can read stories of the Civil War from
a farmer's viewpoint, a slave's viewpoint, a child's
viewpoint, a soldier's viewpoint — and get completely
different outlooks on the same events. Stories involv-
ing World War II were just as varied. I've read stories
about Jews hiding, about Russian children starving,
English people rationing, Americans uniting after
Pearl Harbor, and the list could go on and on.

Vietnam was different. The same theme was in
every book — only minor personal details varied. Usually, an idealistic, resigned, and/or ignorant-of-the-
horrors-of-Vietnam soldier went to war, went through
hell, lost a lot of his sanity and all his innocence, and
came back to a hostile or indifferent society. Even the
terminology was the same from book to book.

And Neil's story was no different. In fact, one
book was so like Neil that it was spooky. Whole sentences were exactly the same as he had related to me.
Even the settings and times were the same.

And so I came to a resignation about why Neil
died. Really, it's a wonder he lived as long as he did.
He really was a survivor in his own way. I think he just
finally depleted his resources with which to cope. I understood now his inability to talk about Vietnam, his
initial confusion about our relationship as friends, his

contempt for the government, and his lack of trust. And I understood his pain. I like to think that God looked down in His infinite mercy on a hurting and desperate Neil and said, "Enough!"

I never finished typing a page that day. I kept typing the same mistake over and over. My frustration mounted until I wanted to heave the typewriter out the window. Instead, I darted into the living room, grabbed my mini-jogger and started jumping with all that was in me. This had become my antidote for anxiety, and I used it often.

THUMP, THUMP, THUMP, my feet said. THUMP, THUMP, THUMP. Neil, I thought to myself, I've got to finish this. I've got to put you behind me. I'm wondering if this preoccupation with you is healthy. I feel like it's driving me crazy.

THUMP, THUMP, THUMP ... Several days earlier, Neil's face had appeared before me, for no reason at all, while I was reading a book about the Civil War. It stayed just long enough to startle me and then was gone. I recalled that experience as I jumped, and I came to the realization that even if I finished his story, it wouldn't be finished for me. I would still be wondering, still be mourning, still be alone in my grief.

THUMP, THUMP, THUMP ... Paradoxically, though my breathing and heartbeat were becoming faster, my stormy disposition was quieting down. Oh Neil, I sighed, what am I going to do with you?

THUMP, THUMP, THUMP ... I was looking at the neighbor's yard across the street through our front window. I wonder why Mrs. Kent's daffodils stand up so tall and straight while mine all kind of keel over, I was thinking. I probably didn't plant mine deep enough. Those gorgeous red flowers on the side of their house sure do add color. Maybe I'll go over and ask her what they are when I'm done here.

"Call the coroner." It was The Voice again. I didn't even break stride. THUMP, THUMP, THUMP ... Not for a moment did I doubt that I'd call, but in my frustration, I wanted some answers first.

I rolled my eyes heavenward. "What am I calling the coroner about now?" I asked out loud. Only my feet answered. THUMP ... THUMP ... THUMP ...

It started to rain — big, blotchy drops, making a pattern on the street and playing music on the roof.

Oh Neil, is it raining on your grave, too? Does anyone bring you flowers? Am I the only one who still remembers you?

Then a thought struck me: He could be buried in Tacoma! He said he had a brother in Tacoma — that's not so far! I think if I could just see his grave, I could put him behind me and find some peace.

THUMP, THUMP, THUMP ... I wonder how a person would go about locating a grave. I feel so morbid, but if I just knew ... and then I laughed. Of course! Call the coroner.

Breathless and sweaty, I looked up the number. It was when the phone started ringing that I became nervous. The same kind voice that I had talked to before answered.

"Uh ... a friend of mine died in September, and it was my understanding that it took a while to locate his family. I'm ... kind of ... uh ... wondering where he's buried."

As he looked up Neil's name, the words, WHAT AM I DOING?!, chanted through my mind over and over and over.

"Well," the coroner said, "I'm afraid the morgue got full, and we sent him over to Skyline Memorial Mortuary. They handle the charity cases. His father was located in North Carolina in November. That's about all the information I have on him."

Before I lost my nerve, I was dialing Skyline. I repeated my story and was put on hold. WHAT AM I DOING? WHAT AM I DOING?!

I was transferred to a different department. Stammering, I repeated my story a third time. It was unnecessary. A very warm female voice told me without hesitation that Neil was buried without funeral at Willamette National Cemetery after his family was located in November.

My eyes filled with tears. Willamette National Cemetery is only five miles south of where we live; we'd gone by it dozens of times and didn't know. All this time I wondered ... and his grave was so near.

"Let's see," she was saying, "date of death is September 28, and ..."

"September 28?" I interrupted. "I was told he died the 26th or 27th."

"Well, sometimes, when he doesn't know exactly when a person has died, if it's only a matter of a few days, the coroner will date it the day he first sees the body. Do you know the family?"

I was still digesting the date of death information. "I ... oh ... uh ... no. I understood they live back East."

Without pause, she read his father's address to me, and I scrambled for a pen to write it down.

"And, I see here that cause of death is just listed as 'accidental.' I guess that's about all the information I have."

I thanked her profusely and hung up. It had been so easy. She didn't think I was weird! She acted like I was entitled to the information!

"There wasn't even a funeral!" I wailed to Logan on the phone a few minutes later.

"Well, maybe his family had a memorial service for him," he suggested. "It costs a lot to ship a body, and Neil could be buried at Willamette free."

That's true, I thought, pacified. Since Neil was a veteran, he could be buried in a national cemetery at no cost. How ironic — the very government Neil despised buried him free.

I cried.

***

Several weeks went by before nice weather and the opportunity to visit Neil's grave came at the same time. Logan and I stopped at the information office at the cemetery to find the location of the grave, and I was surprised at how apprehensive I felt.

When they couldn't find his name, I wearily repeated my well-worn story: He died the last week of September, was in the morgue for a while, was sent over to Skyline until his parents were located in November, and then was buried at Willamette.

"What's his middle name?" I was asked.

"I don't know."

"Could he have been cremated?"

"Uh ... possibly ... I don't know."

"Well," said the cheerful, cherubic lady behind the counter, "let's call Skyline and get this straightened out!"

That call yielded the cause for confusion. Neil's real first name was Cornelius. After that, it wasn't long before I found myself at the end of a row of graves reading:

CORNELIUS P MC CARTHY

PVT U S ARMY

VIETNAM

AUG 29 1950   SEPT 28 1983

I waited for myself to cry, to throw myself on the ground, to feel some kind of strong emotional release. Instead, I stood numbly.

Well, Neil, I thought. I found you. It took me awhile, but I found you ... well, not really you, but what's left of the you that I knew here on earth.

I stood awhile longer, staring at the headstone. You're not here, Neil. I was looking for you to find some peace ... but you just aren't here.

Maybe it was seeing Cornelius. Maybe it was knowing that the Neil I knew was with God and was no longer tied to his body. I don't know. But, it was as if I was looking at a stranger's grave. The feeling I had is much the same that I have when I visit my father's grave — the name is there, but there are no feelings attached to seeing it — good or bad.

"I know," Sharon said when I shared it with her later. "It's like seeing Daddy's name on an envelope or something. I know he's not in that grave, so it means nothing to me."

Well, I thought to myself, as I trudged down the small incline to where our truck was parked, I feel better for knowing where Neil is buried. And it's a pretty place, here. I looked around at the well-kept green grass and the nice view. It was about half-way up Mt. Scott, and I could see part of the city from where we were. The sun was shining, and there wasn't a cloud in the sky. I couldn't have asked for better weather; there was a slight breeze, and the temperature was in the high sixties.

Yes, I felt better. Neil's earthly body was taken care of. But I knew it wasn't the peace I was looking for. I knew Neil's memory would still haunt me. I knew there was something more I had to do. Neil's story was still unfinished.

***

I was sitting on a Greyhound bus, waiting for it to get started. I was in an aisle seat, and someone stepped over me to get to the empty window seat next to me. I didn't look up to see who it was until a hand touched my arm. I looked to see who was there, and it was Neil. I gasped and woke up.

I laid in my bed for several minutes in the dark, trying to sort real from unreal. When my eyes started to make out the outlines of my dresser and the bedroom door, and my heart had stopped its pounding, I threw my arm over my sweaty forehead.

"Oh Neil," I whispered, "Whatever am I going to do with you?"

This was one of several dreams I had been having of Neil. I was fighting a dilemma, and I suppose my dreams were reflecting that struggle. I was aware that I should write his parents, but I was reluctant. I knew I had been praying for some contact with his family, but I thought the answer would come in the form of a letter from them. I thought that perhaps they'd find my address in his effects and contact me. That I would be handed their address on a silver platter, and I would be the one to make the initial contact never occurred to me.

I was afraid. I was ignorant of so much. I didn't know his relationship with them; he had been so secretive and defensive about the whole subject; I didn't know but what he had been cut off from them, or was ignored by them at best. I didn't know why it had taken them so long to learn of his death and how that news had been received. And I didn't want to horn in where perhaps I didn't belong. Most of all, though, I simply didn't know what to write. I couldn't form any words for the message I wanted to convey.

So, for several days I'd try to ignore it all. It's over! I'd tell myself. And then I'd have a dream or see something that reminded me of Neil, and I'd begin the internal fight all over again.

One day, I was rocking Leighton after his nap. He was watching Sesame Street, and I started thinking about Neil's mother. Maybe I'm naive, but I just can't imagine a mother who could be indifferent to her son, no matter his age or what he had done. I looked at Leighton's little legs draped lazily over mine and thought that I'd come near to falling apart if Leighton had died on the other side of the country and I hadn't known for two months. The anguish would be incredible, and it would comfort me to hear from a friend of his. It would help to share that grief.

Several days later, at church, I saw a friend of mine who I hadn't seen in a couple of years since her move to the Seattle area. I was sitting in the foyer, and she came out of the auditorium with her restless young son, and we started catching up on each other. Robyn is the kind of friend with whom you can pick up right where you left off. Without preliminaries, she was telling me about some counseling and painful growth she was experiencing. I, in turn, told her some of what a stay in a psychiatric hospital was like, and I found myself telling her about Neil.

Robyn sat rooted to her seat, oblivious that worship was now over and people were milling all around us. Her eyes never left mine.

When I told her about getting Neil's parents' address, she grabbed my hand and said urgently, "Judy, you must write them!"

At that moment, to the left of Robyn's head, a scene replayed itself. Neil and I were taking our last walk around the block on the day I was discharged from the hospital. We were huffing and puffing, and I heard myself saying, "... I'll always be for you. I'll always be on your side. I may not agree with what you say or do, but that's separate and apart from NEIL ..."

And suddenly I knew that my commitment to Neil didn't end with his death. I had to write his family and help them understand Neil if they didn't already understand him, and help comfort them if they did.

I looked back at Robyn. Her eyes were still boring into mine. "Uh ... yeah," I said, vaguely, "I really must write them. They need to know ..."

But, what was I going to say?

***

It all came together for me the next week on Mother's Day. I was worn out after a busy, hectic morning of calling my own mother and attending church and getting Logan's mother's gift to her and celebrating in general. I was glad for a few quiet hours to celebrate in my own way by taking a nap.

When I woke up, I stretched and enjoyed the bit of sun that was coming through the window. I thought about motherhood in general and about how nebulously SUCCESS is measured. In many ways, being a mother is the hardest work I've ever done.

And then for the first time that day, I thought about Neil's mother. What a painful day this must be for her! And the sad part is, she has nothing to be ashamed of. Neil was so good, so proper...

The words started coming so fast, I grabbed a pen and paper, and in five minutes I had my message to Neil's family written:

Dear Mr. and Mrs. McCarthy,

I want you to know that I'm very sorry to hear about Neil's death.

I knew Neil only the last couple of months of his life, but I always found him to be very considerate, po-

lite, and proper in everything he did. I remember think-
ing at the time that a person could tell he had been
raised right.

Neil was very reticent about his family, and I
honored his desire for privacy. But I gathered that you
hadn't seen him in a long while. It distresses me to think
that all you may know of Neil's last days were his con-
fusion and depression — because there was so much
more to Neil than that. He was very good and kind and
eager to be better. Certainly, he was somewhat rough
around the edges, but he excelled in the things that re-
ally mattered. He was a good friend, and I miss him
greatly.

I'm sorry for the delay in writing you; it took me
awhile to catch up with what happened and to whom I
should write.

Please know that I share your sorrow.
Sincerely,

Ah! I thought to myself as I mailed it the next
day. Peace! I did the right thing. Now I can get on with
living and put Neil behind me.

Relief? Yes. Freedom from dreams of Neil? Yes.
Rest from indecision? Yes. But, peace? No.

I got an answer a month later.

***

I had about given up on an answer, so when the
mailman came that afternoon, I finished my lunch and
put Leighton down for a nap before I went to the mail-
box just outside our front door.

When I saw McCarthy on the envelope, I dropped the other mail at my feet and tore it open, my breathing coming fast.

Dear Judy,

Mr. McCarthy, myself and family are very appreciative of your consideration in writing to us concerning Neil's death. It is always healing to hear from a friend such as yourself and to know that you miss him too.

We learned of Neil's death on Nov. 9, 83, through a thoughtful friend of Neil's. He realized we had never been notified. This has been very hurtful to all the family. Thoughts of the anxiety overwhelms me.

Neil was dearly loved by the family and we kept in close touch but our hurt is that Neil was too proud to realize how much we wanted him to remain here and let us help him back to health.

What Neil had to offer is so badly needed in the world. My husband and I are hoping somehow to manage a trip to Portland, Oregon in the next year. I would be glad to meet with you.

Sincerely,
Connie McCarthy

I crossed the room and flopped on the couch. My initial reaction was relief — relief that my message had been favorably received; relief that Neil had been loved by his family; relief that I wasn't alone in my grief anymore; and relief that I had gotten a response at all.

But the more I read the letter, the more I knew with mounting apprehension that some issues had to be addressed, and that I'd have to write yet another letter.

First of all, the pain seemed to leap off the page at me. And it wasn't pain that was confined to the grief that her son had died. That was something I could do nothing about at that point; I'd already expressed my condolences.

Rather, the pain was two-pronged: It sounded to me as if she thought he might have committed suicide. She certainly sounded ignorant of the details of his death at best. Also, she was hurt at what she considered Neil's pride that kept him from accepting her help, implying that the breach with his family was one-sided. I had to make an effort to help her understand that it may not have been pride, but Neil's depression that drove a wedge between them. Her anguish about that and the circumstances surrounding his death may be needless.

I also wanted to let her know I'd be glad to meet her. I wanted to know this person who had raised Neil. I wanted to share with her a side of Neil she may not have known or had been too hurt to see or remember. I wanted her to be proud to be Neil's mother and not to be crippled by memories of a tragic life and wonder what she could have done to make it different.

In the days that followed, I did what I had done before — tried to forget, avoided the issue; put everything on the back burner. But the nights brought it all back. If I wasn't pacing the floor, wondering how I'd gotten so strongly involved in all this, I was having dreams and nightmares. After a week, I decided I'd write again, even if I made a fool of myself.

Since Neil had told me he came from a Catholic family, I knew that death by suicide would have serious ramifications in the grieving process of his family.

I wasn't sure what they were, specifically, but it seemed to me that if for no other reason, I should write to let them know there was no sign of suicide. I decided to wait on writing until I saw Dr. Larsen again. I didn't want to write her and then learn that a suicide note had been found later. I wanted to review my facts with him and confirm that nothing had changed concerning the way he died.

Meanwhile, I made up an outline of the points I wanted to make, thinking that I'd write the letter and when I saw the doctor, I'd just mail it, provided Dr. Larsen gave me the "no-suicide" information.

But no words came. Writing had been so easy before ... maybe this wasn't the right time. I'd try again ... nothing. My pen point sat motionless on the paper, my mind a blank. Hmmmm ... okay, I'll wait until I see Dr. Larsen, I reasoned. Maybe that'll inspire me.

Three weeks later, the day before my appointment with the doctor, I got a phone call that was to change the pace of my thinking. It was from a girl who had been a close friend of Logan's brother, Chris, in the early 1970's. She had lost contact with Chris when he moved to California, and she was intending to call all the Cowarts in the phone book to learn his whereabouts.

So, it fell to me to tell her that Chris had died five years earlier in a plane crash. I heard first a squeaky, "Oh!" and then crying. I filled in the awkward moments by volunteering the details of his death, but there came a time when I'd said about all I could say.

"I'm sorry," she'd say and then cry some more.

"It's okay," I said over and over, my eyes filling and refilling with tears. And then, suddenly, it wasn't

Chris' friend crying, but Neil's mother. It seemed to be in stereo all over the room. Goose bumps stood out on my arms as I looked around the room, disbelieving that the rush of sound I was hearing was confined to the phone.

"You're not going to believe this," the girl was saying, "but I had a dream about Chris last night. He was dressed all in white; it was like white sparklers were all around him, and he was telling me it was all right — that the best was yet to be — to just hang in there. You see, I'm going through a real rough time now, and I thought if I could just talk to Chris again ... but now I know why I had that dream.

"I'm not particularly religious," she went on, "but I just know he's in a better place. Oh, I don't know why I'm telling you this. You must think I'm crazy, but I'm ..."

"No, no;" I broke in, chuckling ruefully. "I understand, really I do."

We wound up the conversation, exchanging our memories of Chris. After I hung up, I felt a great urgency: HURRY, HURRY. I heard the crying all over again and felt the need to write Neil's mother right away.

For two hours I labored. It was warm that day, and sweat ran unimpeded down the sides of my face. I stopped to throw together some dinner, noticing that Leighton had been up from his nap for some time, since toys were strewn from one end of the house to the other. But for once, I didn't care.

That evening, I ended up the letter, heedless that the Olympics were on television just a few feet from me. I read the letter over, but I wasn't happy with it.

In the middle of the night, I sat up in bed with a gasp. If I had had a dream, I didn't remember it, but I could hear the familiar sobbing echoing away. I looked at my digital clock and read 3:12. I looked over at Logan, just making him out in the dim light. I could hear his deep, steady breathing and was relieved that I hadn't disturbed him. Sighing, I got up to wash my sweating face and to somehow erase the unrest I felt.

Oh Lord, I thought as I looked at myself in the mirror, now <u>my</u> eyes look haunted.

I wandered into the spare bedroom where I had left the rough draft of the letter. I scratched out a sentence and inserted another. I paced about and then fell onto the couch in frustration.

"God," I prayed aloud, "what's the big deal? Why did the words come so easily before and now I'm stuttering so? Please let me rest. I promise I'll mail the letter tomorrow, only please just give me some direction in this. Am I doing the right thing?"

My mind was as blank as the ceiling I was staring at. I finally got up, took some Xanax, and went back to bed.

The next morning, at the end of the visit with Dr. Larsen, I broached the subject of Neil's mother's letter. No, nothing had changed as far as he knew. Neil had had almost a full bottle of anti-depressants left. If he had wanted to die, it seemed reasonable that he would have taken more than three or four. Dr. Larsen expressed regret that the family hadn't contacted him, but I told him I didn't think they knew how he died, much less who his doctor was.

On the way home, Logan and I stopped by the cemetery. I stared at Neil's headstone, still wet from the sprinklers that were watering the lawn, and I silently pleaded: Tell me what to say, Neil! What am I going to write your mother?

But there was no answer. He wasn't there.

When I got home, the HURRY, HURRY had intensified. Sounds of weeping dogged my steps. I am really going bonkers, I told myself as I scrambled for pen, paper, and the rough draft of the letter. For the next half-hour I wrote, improvising as I went along.

Dear Mrs. McCarthy,

Thank you very much for your letter. Of course, I would be most glad to meet with you whenever you and your husband can come to Portland. I would very much like to share with you the Neil that I knew.

I am relieved to know that Neil was loved by his family. My heart very often went out to him — he seemed so alone in the world; it is comforting to know that his family cared for him.

I know that trust came very slowly for Neil. He was depressed; and just as a fever and congestion are a part of pneumonia, so is withdrawing and a pushing away of support and love a part of depression. Somehow, depression plays tricks with the mind in how one sees reality, and it's real easy to feel that others don't understand and are even against you. I know that in our friendship, he often pulled back with what I thought was undue caution, which was confusing to me at times. I don't pretend to have known Neil better than you did, nor am I aware of the specifics of your relationship with him, but perhaps it would bring you some comfort to consider Neil's rejection of your desire to help him as a part of his depression. Maybe his illness prevented him from accepting your help — maybe it wasn't Neil talking, but his depression preventing him from feeling the support that was there. I know that must have been painful for you.

How tragic to have learned of Neil's death so long after he died. I know how stunned I was — how much worse it must have been for you. I don't know much of the details surrounding his death, but I was somewhat consoled to learn that there was no sign of suicide. The coroner listed it as accidental, since there were only about three or four anti-depressants in his body. Neil was troubled by insomnia, and since his medication helped him to sleep, it was assumed he took more than the prescribed dosage to help him get some rest. There was also some alcohol in his system which enhanced the effect the pills had on his nervous system, and he simply stopped breathing. I know that the last time I saw Neil, he was optimistic and had a lot of carefully laid plans for the future. I don't know how much you know of how Neil died — I'm offering this information to comfort you, because I know he wanted to live.

Neil is buried in a cemetery only about five miles from where we live. I've been up there a couple of times, and it's very pretty and peaceful there. It's a small military cemetery about halfway up a large hill, and they keep it up very nicely.

I want you to know that you have every reason to be proud of Neil. He was one of those rare individuals who was genuinely good; it was second nature for him to be honorable and respectful. I was so impressed by

his courtesy and kindness. Even though he was in des-
pair much of the time, he had a delightful sense of hu-
mor and a very sensitive spirit. I hope you can remem-
ber Neil for all the bright, happy times you had with
him, and not so much for how he died and the circum-
stances surrounding his death. He just died as the re-
sult of an illness, that's all, and I'll always remember
Neil as young and vital and good.

If there is anything I can do to ease your grief,
please, I want to do it. Just let me know.
                    Sincerely,

I was stamping the letter when the mailman
came. As he took it away, I thought: Well, there it goes,
for better or for worse; it's on its way. Did I do the right
thing? Did I say the words that will aid in some healing? Did God truly work through me in this? Will she
accept it as it was meant?

I didn't know. But I spent the whole afternoon
sleeping, dreamless, in utter exhaustion.

***

And so now I've come full circle. It's been a year
since Neil died; nearly two months since I last wrote
his mother.

A couple of weeks ago, this thought hit me with
a jolt: Neil is dead. I will never see him on this earth
again.

I have lived with this book, and Neil has shown
up in my dreams and thoughts so often this past year
that I've lost track of the fact that his life here on earth
is ended.

I still startle when I read or hear his name attached to someone else. I cried through most of "The Jazz Singer" when I saw it on television recently, because physically, Neil Diamond, who played the lead, favors Neil so very much, even down to his slight Eastern accent. Sometimes, too, I'm just lonely for Neil's friendship.

And what is perhaps more surprising than my reaction to this first thought is that I'm not sad about it, because, I suppose, to me, he will always be alive. Maybe that's what the Apostle Paul meant when he said: *"Brothers, we do not want you to be ignorant about those who sleep, or to grieve like the rest of men, who have no hope. We believe that Jesus died and rose again and so we believe that God will bring with Jesus those who sleep in him." (1 Thess. 4:13-14)*

And I understand for the first time what some Jews believe when they say we achieve eternal life by living on in others. Though some feel no hope of a reunion in Christ and that's tragic, it is true that we do touch each other's lives in such a way that we all live on and on, even after we're physically dead.

And I think I've found the key to setting to rest all the mixed feelings and inner turmoil that began when I met Neil and intensified when he died. My mistake in dealing with the after-effects of Neil's death was trying to say goodbye, or at the very least, putting him behind me. Now I know I can't and never will; nor — surprise! — do I want to. I'll still think of him when I watch a football game, or see a shock of unruly dark hair, or read a story of Vietnam and its consequences. I've accepted the fact that I'll probably still have dreams about him and cry over war and depression and V.A. hospitals.

But, I don't have to fight that anymore. That was a part of Neil that, because I tend to soak up others' emotions and problems like a sponge, became a part of me. And the other side of the coin, the positive side, is that I soaked up his example of courage, gentleness, and steadfastness, even in the face of pain and disappointment and fear. That became a part of me, too.

The other day, I looked up the meaning of the name, Neil. I chuckled as I read it: "Champion." It has been said: "To die without realizing one's ambitions is part of the human tragedy; but to die still trying is heroism." Neil fought, he struggled, he made mistakes, fell, and got up again for thirteen years. But in the end, God took him to Himself. It was a long journey home.

Welcome, Champion.